Council of Academic Societies
Spring Meeting
March 23-26, 2000
Savannah, Georgia

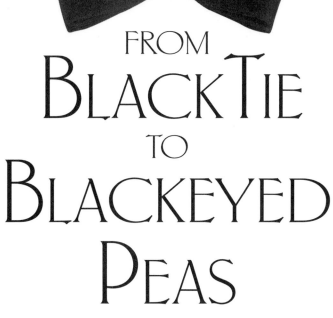

FROM
BLACK TIE
TO
BLACKEYED
PEAS

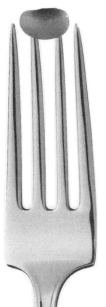

S A V A N N A H ' S   S A V O R Y   S E C R E T S

Copyright 2000
St. Joseph's Foundation of Savannah, Inc.
11705 Mercy Boulevard
Savannah, Georgia 31419
912-927-5117

Library of Congress Number: 99-071397
ISBN: 0-9671621-0-6

Designed, Edited, and Manufactured by
Favorite Recipes® Press
an imprint of

FRP™

P.O. Box 305142
Nashville, Tennessee 37230
1-800-358-0560

Book Design: David Malone
Art Director: Steve Newman
Project Manager: Susan Larson

Manufactured in the United States of America
First Printing: 2000   12,500 copies

The Wormsloe Plantation

Constructed by Noble Jones, one of Georgia's first settlers, Wormsloe Plantation may have been named Wormsloe in honor of the silkworms he hoped to cultivate. A fortification was constructed between 1739 and 1745 to protect the inland water approach to Savannah against Spanish attacks from the south. Remains of the fort can still be viewed from the river. The beautiful gate marks the entrance to the plantation and the beginning of a 1.5-mile avenue of live oaks that was planted in the 1890s.

TABLE OF CONTENTS

Preface

My interest in food, and more especially cooking, stems from my early childhood. My mother had in her employ a cook by the name of Mattie Williams. Mattie was truly a jewel and could do things with food that even Escoffier would have problems doing. Although most of her dishes were Low Country style, they had a flair that would "knock your socks off." During my grammar school years, she insisted that I learn to cook, and said, "You never know when you'll have to cook for yourself." She was so right. She was the one who planted the seed that has grown with me over the rest of my life. This wonderful cookbook, *From Black Tie to Blackeyed Peas: Savannah's Savory Secrets,* epitomizes good food, good tested recipes, and "good food for thought." I'm especially pleased with the format and the descriptive material. It will be a great help and value to the occasional cook, as well as the seasoned chef. Savannah cuisine is unique unto itself, as the title of the cookbook so aptly implies. From the wonderful fresh *fruits de mer* such as crab, shrimp, oysters, and clams, one may prepare local seafood dishes, as well as meat and poultry entreés, turnip greens, Savannah Red Rice, and yes, even Hoppin' John. The contributors are to be complimented, and I know that you will enjoy having your copy close at hand.

Laissez le bon temps roulé—bon appétit.

Irving Victor, M.D., F.A.C.S.
Vice President, Medical Affairs

INTRODUCTION

Savannah's hospitality has not changed since William Gaston was president of the Planter's Bank during the heyday of the cotton boom. He was known both for his philanthropy and generosity as a host. It was said that no stranger came to Savannah who was not welcome at Mr. Gaston's bountiful board. Upon his death in 1837, his friends decided that the "Stranger's Tomb" should be built to perpetuate his spirit of hospitality. This was a place where visitors who died in Savannah were placed awaiting transfer to their home communities. Gaston, the generous host to the living, would now be the silent host to the recently departed.

The Gaston spirit lives today in this vibrant city known as the "Hostess City of the South." Now our vintage cooks have shared their savory secrets *From Black Tie to Blackeyed Peas.* This collection of recipes takes you on a stroll through historic Savannah from Savory Beginnings to secret endings.

Many thanks to all the friends who have contributed to this book. *From Black Tie to Blackeyed Peas* is dedicated to all patients who have received the "spirit of mercy" since the founding of St. Joseph's Hospital in 1875.

Karen C. Davis

Karen C. Davis, Director
St. Joseph's Foundation of Savannah, Inc.

Special Thanks

Georgia Historical Society

Historic Savannah Foundation

Dr. Christopher Hendricks
Armstrong Atlantic State University
History Department

Wanda Scott

Monica McGoldrick

Angela Brackett

Helen Marie Fleming

Judy Freeman

Bev Britt

Georgia Department of Agriculture

UGA Cooperative Extension Service
(Vegetable & Fruit Growers Association)

Mayor Floyd B. Adams

Elizabeth on 37th

Charles J. Russo Seafood

FROM

CHEESE BALLS

TO

DAIQUIRIS

SAVORY BEGINNINGS

THE
DAVENPORT
HOUSE

A DINNER PARTY IN 1822

In 1822, Jeremiah Evarts, a lawyer and publisher from New England, came to the warmer climes of Savannah for his health. Soon after his arrival he was invited to the home of Dr. Henry Kollock, minister of Independent Presbyterian Church. Evarts reluctantly agreed to attend, having been assured that it would "be a plain dinner without company and without ceremony." He was not quite prepared for what a simple Savannah meal would entail.

The first course of the dinner consisted of "fish, with appropriate dressings, ducks, and southern bacon, oysters cooked in two ways, Irish potatoes in two ways, beets, onions, bread and boiled rice." Once the guests had finished eating, servants removed the serving pieces and place settings and replaced them with settings and "cherry-pye, cranberry-pye, quince (an Asian fruit like apple), orange and other preserves, with sallad, cheese, butter, and cream (beat to a foam with the flavor from juice of pineapple)." Beverages during the first course may have included water, beer, and light wines. Between courses, people frequently drank champagne. After dinner, when the ladies had withdrawn into a parlor, liquors and red wines would have been served.

After his experience at Dr. Kollock's home, a surprised Evarts remarked, "Yet this was a dinner made for invalids: the luxury of this city, as exhibited at dinners, is very great."

"...the luxury of this city, as exhibited at dinners, is very great."

Feay Shellman Coleman, *Nostrums for Fashionable Entertainments: Dining in Georgia 1800–1850.* Savannah, Georgia: Telfair Academy of Arts and Sciences, Incorporated, 1992.

CAVALIER CHEESE BALL

This is a wonderful cheese ball. A favorite that never fails to please!

8 ounces cream cheese, softened
8 ounces bleu cheese
1/4 cup butter, softened
2/3 cup chopped black olives

1 tablespoon snipped chives
1/3 cup chopped walnuts or pecans

Combine the cream cheese, bleu cheese and butter in a bowl and mix well. Stir in the olives and chives. Shape into a ball. Roll in the walnuts to coat. Refrigerate, covered, until completely chilled. Place on a serving plate. Serve with crackers.

Yield: 12 servings

PALMETTO CHEESE APPETIZER

1 2/3 cups Cheddar cheese cracker crumbs
3 tablespoons butter or margarine, melted
2 cups sour cream
3 hard-cooked eggs, finely chopped
3 garlic cloves, crushed, or 1 garlic clove, minced

1/4 cup finely chopped green bell pepper
3 tablespoons lemon juice
1/2 teaspoon Beau Monde seasoning
1/4 teaspoon salt
1 teaspoon Worcestershire sauce
1/2 teaspoon paprika
Dash of hot sauce

Combine the cracker crumbs and butter in a bowl and mix well. Press 1/3 of the crumbs over the bottom of a greased 8-inch springform pan. Combine the sour cream, eggs, garlic, bell pepper, lemon juice, Beau Monde seasoning, salt, Worcestershire sauce, paprika and hot sauce in a bowl and mix well. Layer the sour cream mixture and remaining crumb mixture 1/2 at a time over the crumb layer. Decorate with a palmetto frond. Remove the side of the pan and place on a serving plate. Serve with cut vegetables or party crackers.

Yield: 10 servings

CHRISTMAS TERRINE

32 ounces cream cheese, softened

2 teaspoons Tabasco sauce

2 (9-ounce) jars sun-dried tomato spread

2 envelopes unflavored gelatin

1/2 cup cold water

1 (7-ounce) jar pesto

1/2 cup butter, softened

1 garlic clove, pressed

2 teaspoons fresh cracked pepper

1 teaspoon basil

2 tablespoons lemon juice

2 teaspoons herbes de Provence

1 teaspoon green Tabasco sauce

2 teaspoons dried chives

Line the sides and bottom of a 5x9-inch loaf pan with plastic wrap, allowing a small amount of overhang at the top. Combine 8 ounces of the cream cheese with the Tabasco sauce and the tomato spread in a bowl and mix well. Soften 1 envelope of the gelatin in 1/4 cup of the cold water. Microwave for 1 minute or until dissolved. Stir into the tomato mixture. Spread over the bottom of the loaf pan. Chill for 1 hour or until firm. Soften the remaining gelatin in the remaining 1/4 cup cold water. Microwave for 1 minute or until dissolved. Combine the dissolved gelatin and pesto in a bowl and mix well. Spread over the tomato layer. Chill until firm. Combine the remaining 24 ounces cream cheese and butter in a bowl and mix well. Add the garlic, pepper, basil, lemon juice, herbes de Provence, green Tabasco sauce and chives and mix well. Spread over the pesto layer. Chill, covered, for 4 hours or until firm. Unmold onto a bed of chopped red lettuce, black olives or pickled okra on a serving plate. Garnish with chopped parsley. Serve with crackers.

Yield: 12 servings

GARDEN POTATO DIP

2 cups firmly packed frozen mashed potatoes, thawed

1 cup milk

1/2 cup ranch salad dressing

1/2 cup chopped plum tomatoes

1/2 cup chopped red, orange and/or yellow bell peppers

1/4 cup chopped pitted kalamata or ripe olives

1/4 cup chopped red onion or chives

1/4 teaspoon salt, or to taste

1/4 teaspoon pepper, or to taste

Prepare the potatoes in a microwave-safe bowl according to package directions using 1 cup milk. Microwave for 6 minutes. Stir in the remaining ingredients. Spoon into a serving bowl. Refrigerate, covered, for 2 hours or longer. Serve with pita or bagel chips and fresh vegetables.

Yield: 12 servings

CORNMEAL CUPS FILLED WITH BLACK BEAN SALSA

From The Butler Agency

6 tablespoons butter, softened
3 ounces cream cheese, softened
1 cup flour
$^{1}/_{2}$ cup cornmeal
$^{1}/_{2}$ cup chopped oregano
Black Bean Salsa

Cream the butter and cream cheese in a bowl until light and fluffy. Add the flour, cornmeal and oregano and mix well. Shape into 1-inch balls. Press into small muffin cups, molding to the cup; pastry should be even and come up to the rim. Bake at 350 degrees for 20 minutes or until brown. Cool in the pan for 10 minutes. Remove to a wire rack to cool completely. Fill with Black Bean Salsa.

Yield: 2$^{1}/_{2}$ dozen

BLACK BEAN SALSA

2 (15-ounce) cans black beans, drained
3 to 4 garlic cloves, chopped
4 to 6 tablespoons grated fresh ginger
$^{1}/_{2}$ cup chopped onion
$^{1}/_{2}$ cup chopped celery
Juice of 1 lemon
Salt and pepper to taste

Purée 1$^{1}/_{2}$ cups of the beans in a blender. Combine the puréed beans, remaining beans, garlic, ginger, onion and celery in a bowl and mix well. Stir in the lemon juice. Season with salt and pepper.

The Pirate's House is a modest frame structure with blue shutters (to keep the haunts away). Often during the rum bouts, while notorious river pirates mingled with sailors from all over the world, drugged and drunken seamen were dragged off and shanghaied onto waiting vessels, waking to find themselves on the high seas bound for some exotic port. One Savannah policeman stopped by the Pirate's House for a friendly drink and awoke on a four-masted schooner bound for China. It took him two years to make his way back to Savannah.

Betsy Fancher—Book, *Savannah: A Renaissance of the Heart*

HERITAGE CRAB SPREAD

3 teaspoons grated onion
6 ounces cream cheese, softened
1 tablespoon mayonnaise
1 tablespoon Worcestershire sauce

1 teaspoon lemon juice
Cocktail sauce to taste
1 cup fresh crab meat

Combine the onion, cream cheese, mayonnaise, Worcestershire sauce and lemon juice in a bowl and mix well. Shape into a loaf and place on a serving dish. Pour enough cocktail sauce over the loaf to cover it. Sprinkle with the crab meat. Refrigerate, covered, until ready to serve. Serve with crackers.

Yield: 8 servings

CREAMY HOT CRAB DIP

8 ounces cream cheese, softened
1 tablespoon dry white wine or vermouth
2 tablespoons chopped onion
$1/2$ teaspoon white horseradish

$1/4$ teaspoon salt
$1/8$ teaspoon pepper
8 ounces lump crab meat
$1/4$ cup almonds

Preheat oven to 375 degrees. Combine the cream cheese and wine in a bowl and stir until well blended. Add the onion, horseradish, salt and pepper and mix well. Fold in the crab meat. Spoon into a small shallow baking dish. Sprinkle the almonds over the top. Bake for 15 minutes or until the almonds are brown and the mixture is hot and bubbly. Serve hot.

Yield: 8 to 10 servings

BAKED CRAB, BRIE AND ARTICHOKE DIP

From Susan Mason Catering

1 medium leek, white part only

1/2 cup drained canned artichoke hearts

1/2 cup thawed frozen chopped spinach

1 pound Brie cheese

1 medium Vidalia or sweet onion of choice, finely chopped

2 tablespoons minced garlic

2 tablespoons olive oil

1/4 cup Riesling or medium-dry white wine of choice

2/3 cup whipping cream

3 tablespoons finely chopped fresh parsley leaves

2 tablespoons finely chopped fresh dill leaves

1 tablespoon finely chopped fresh tarragon leaves

1 pound fresh jumbo lump crab meat

1 teaspoon mustard

1 teaspoon Tabasco sauce or to taste

Salt and pepper to taste

Preheat oven to 425 degrees. Trim and finely chop the leek. Rinse the chopped leek in a large bowl of water; drain. Rinse and finely chop the artichoke hearts. Squeeze the spinach between paper towels to remove excess moisture. Finely chop the spinach. Remove the rind from the Brie cheese. Cut into 1/4-inch pieces. Cook the leek, onion and garlic in the olive oil in a heavy skillet over medium heat until light golden brown, stirring constantly. Stir in the artichoke hearts and spinach. Pour in the wine. Cook for 3 minutes, stirring constantly. Pour in the cream. Simmer for 1 minute, stirring constantly. Add the cheese. Cook until the cheese begins to melt, stirring constantly. Remove from heat. Stir in the parsley, dill and tarragon. Remove shells from crab meat. Combine the crab meat, mustard, Tabasco sauce, salt and pepper in a bowl and mix well. Stir in the Brie cheese mixture. Spread evenly in a greased 11-inch shallow baking dish. Bake in the center of the oven for 15 to 20 minutes or until golden brown. Serve with toasted thin baguette slices.

Yield: 6 to 8 servings

Georgia alone produces nearly half of the total U.S. supply of peanuts, making it the nation's largest peanut-producing state. Peanuts have been a part of Georgia's rich agricultural heritage since Colonial Days. They helped sustain Union and Confederate troops during the Civil War and, in the years since, have come to be known as one of the most nutritious foods known to mankind. Pound for pound, they contain more protein than milk, eggs, and most popular meats.

White Bluff Shrimp Paste

8 ounces cream cheese, softened

1 tablespoon lemon juice

1/4 teaspoon onion powder

Dash of hot sauce

Pinch of mace

Dash of garlic salt

Dash of onion salt

1 cup finely chopped cooked shrimp

Chopped parsley or toasted sesame seeds (optional)

Combine the cream cheese, lemon juice, onion powder, hot sauce, mace, garlic salt and onion salt in a bowl and mix well. Stir in the shrimp. Shape into a ball. Roll in the chopped parsley to coat. Serve with crackers or on bread slices.

Yield: 4 servings

Black Tie Cocktail Puffs

Pinch of salt

1/2 cup flour

1/2 cup water

1/4 cup butter

2 eggs

Sift the salt and flour together. Bring the water to a boil in a saucepan. Add the butter. Cook until the butter melts. Add the sifted dry ingredients. Cook until the dough forms a ball and leaves the side of the pan, stirring constantly; cool slightly. Add the eggs 1 at a time, beating until the dough is smooth, glossy and fairly stiff. Drop by teaspoonfuls 2-inches apart onto greased baking sheets; do not allow to touch. Bake at 400 degrees for 10 minutes. Reduce heat to 300 degrees. Bake for 20 to 25 minutes or until golden brown and dry. May remove the top and fill with chicken or shrimp salad.

Yield: 70 small puffs

Phyllo Bites

6 long thick asparagus spears, trimmed	6 sheets phyllo dough
Salt to taste	3 tablespoons unsalted butter, melted
Freshly ground pepper	1/2 cup grated Parmesan cheese
9 thin slices lean prosciutto	Freshly grated nutmeg

Preheat oven to 400 degrees. Blanch the asparagus spears in boiling salted water in a saucepan for 2 minutes or until tender-crisp; drain. Rinse in cold water. Pat dry with paper towels. Season with pepper. Cut 3 of the prosciutto slices into halves. Roll each asparagus spear in 1 1/2 slices of prosciutto. Brush 1 sheet of the phyllo dough with melted butter. Sprinkle with 1 tablespoon of the Parmesan cheese and a pinch of nutmeg. Place the wrapped asparagus on the short end of the phyllo sheet and roll it up. Brush the roll with butter. Sprinkle with additional cheese. Place on a baking sheet. Repeat for remaining asparagus spears. Bake on the top shelf of the oven for 10 to 12 minutes or until golden brown and crisp. Remove to a wire rack to cool slightly. Slice at an angle into bite-size pieces.

Yield: 6 servings

Marinated Asparagus with Pecans

2 pounds fresh asparagus, trimmed, or 3 (10-ounce) packages frozen asparagus, thawed	1/4 cup sugar
	1/4 cup white vinegar
	2 tablespoons vegetable oil
	1/4 cup finely chopped pecans
2 tablespoons water	Lettuce leaves

Place the asparagus in a microwave-safe 9x13-inch dish. Sprinkle with 2 tablespoons water. Microwave on High for 5 to 7 minutes or until tender-crisp; drain. Rinse in cold water. Return to the dish. Combine the sugar, vinegar, oil and pecans in a bowl and mix well. Pour over the asparagus. Refrigerate, covered, for 8 hours or longer. Drain, reserving the marinade. Arrange the asparagus over lettuce on individual plates. Drizzle with the reserved marinade.

Yield: 6 to 8 servings

In November 1732 the *Anne* sailed for the New World with James Oglethorpe, some 114 colonists, and—as the press reported—"on Board 10 Ton of Alderman Parsons" . . . "best beer."

Page 17, Excerpt from Edward Chang Sieg, *Eden on the Marsh: An Illustrated History of Savannah*, 1985. Windsor Publications.

Montgomery Spinach Squares

2 (10-ounce) packages frozen chopped spinach, thawed
3 tablespoons butter
1 medium onion, chopped
4 ounces mushrooms, sliced
4 eggs, beaten
1/4 cup fine dry bread crumbs

1 (10-ounce) can cream of mushroom soup
1/4 cup grated Parmesan cheese
1/8 teaspoon pepper
1/8 teaspoon oregano
1/8 teaspoon basil

Press the spinach between paper towels to remove excess moisture. Melt the butter in a skillet. Add the onion and mushrooms. Cook until the onion is tender, stirring frequently. Combine the eggs, bread crumbs, soup, 2 tablespoons of the cheese, pepper, oregano, basil and spinach in a bowl and mix well. Stir in the onion mixture. Spoon into a greased 9-inch square baking pan. Sprinkle with the remaining cheese. Bake at 325 degrees until set. Cool completely. Cut into 1-inch squares. Serve cold.

Yield: 80 squares

Cheese Soufflé Sandwiches

1 pound butter, softened
4 (5-ounce) jars Old English cheese, softened
1 teaspoon onion powder
1 1/2 teaspoons Worcestershire sauce

1 teaspoon Tabasco sauce
1 teaspoon Beau Monde seasoning
1 1/2 teaspoons dillweed
2 1/2 (16-ounce) loaves thin-sliced bread, crusts removed

Beat the butter and cheese in a mixer bowl until light and fluffy. Beat in the onion powder, Worcestershire sauce, Tabasco sauce, Beau Monde seasoning and dillweed. Spread 3 slices of bread with cheese mixture. Stack the slices. Cut into 4 to 6 pieces. Spread the sides with the cheese mixture. Repeat the process with the remaining bread and cheese mixture. Sandwiches may be frozen at this point and thawed before baking. Bake at 325 degrees for 10 to 15 minutes or until edges are brown.

Yield: 65 to 100 sandwiches

Vidalia Onion Sandwiches

These sandwiches can be made the day before serving. They are delicious!

White bread slices   Mayonnaise
Butter or margarine   Chopped parsley
Vidalia onions, thinly sliced   Pimentos

Cut the bread slices into small rounds with a cookie cutter. Spread each round with butter. Place an onion slice over the butter on each bread round. Top with a bread round. Spread mayonnaise on the edge of the sandwich. Roll the edge in parsley to coat. Top each sandwich with a slice of pimento shaped into a bow.

Yield: Variable

Miss Lucille's Tomato Sandwiches

White and whole wheat bread,   Pepper to taste
thinly sliced   MSG to taste
Mayonnaise   Tomatoes, peeled, sliced
Grated onion to taste   Seasoned salt to taste

Cut the bread slices into circles with a doughnut cutter. Remove the center hole. Combine mayonnaise, onion, pepper and MSG to taste in a bowl and mix well. Spread over the bread circles. Refrigerate, covered, for 24 hours. Drain the tomatoes between paper towels. Sprinkle with seasoned salt. Place 1 tomato slice on a prepared whole wheat bread circle. Top with a prepared white bread circle. Refrigerate, covered with a damp tea towel, until ready to serve.

Yield: Variable

TORTILLA ROLLS

8 ounces cream cheese, softened

1 envelope ranch dressing mix

1 (10-count) package flour tortillas

1 red bell pepper, chopped

1 green bell pepper, chopped

3 to 4 ribs celery, chopped

1 (4-ounce) can chopped black olives, drained

Snipped fresh chives to taste

Combine the cream cheese and dressing mix in a bowl and mix well. Spread evenly on each tortilla. Sprinkle the red pepper, green pepper, celery, olives and chives over the cream cheese mixture. Roll up. Refrigerate, covered, for 4 hours or longer. Cut into bite-size pieces. Arrange on a serving platter and serve with salsa.

Yield: 10 servings

RED-HOT WAFERS

1 cup butter or margarine, softened

2 cups shredded Cheddar cheese

2 cups flour

1 teaspoon salt

2 teaspoons cayenne

3 dashes of hot pepper sauce

2 cups finely chopped pecans

Mix the butter and cheese in a bowl Stir in the flour, salt, cayenne and hot pepper sauce. Stir in the pecans. Refrigerate, covered, until dough is firm. Shape into small balls and place on baking sheets. Press each dough ball with a fork. Bake at 350 degrees for 10 minutes or until the wafers are slightly browned. Remove to a wire rack to cool completely. Store in an airtight container or freeze.

Yield: 40 to 50 wafers

APRICOT WINE

Wash and dry 1 pound dried apricots thoroughly. Place in a large crock. Dissolve $1/2$ cake yeast in $1/2$ cup warm water in a bowl. Add a scant gallon warm water. Stir in $6^1/2$ cups sugar, $2^1/4$ cups packed brown sugar, $1^1/2$ cups raisins, 2 lemons and 2 oranges, both thinly sliced, and 1 tablespoon chopped gingerroot. Stir in the dissolved yeast. Cover and let stand for 30 days, stirring every other day. Strain the mixture and bottle.

Ginger and Curry Beef-Filled Phyllo Triangles

From The Butler Agency

1 onion, finely chopped

3 garlic cloves, chopped

$1/4$ cup butter

2 to 4 tablespoons curry powder

2 to 4 teaspoons fresh grated ginger

Salt and pepper to taste

$3/4$ teaspoon cayenne

1 pound ground beef

$1/2$ cup cooked chopped spinach

$1/2$ cup cooked wild rice

1 (16-ounce) package phyllo dough

1 cup clarified butter

Sauté the onion and garlic in the $1/4$ cup butter in a skillet over medium heat until tender. Stir in the curry powder, ginger, salt, pepper and cayenne. Add the ground beef. Cook until browned, stirring until crumbly; drain. Stir in the spinach and rice. Remove from heat. Place 1 sheet of phyllo on work surface. Keep the remaining dough covered with plastic wrap or a slightly damp towel until ready to use. Brush the phyllo sheet with the clarified butter. Place a second sheet of phyllo over the first sheet. Brush with butter. Repeat the process until all the ingredients are used. Cut into 8 equal strips from the long side. Place 1 teaspoon of filling at the top of each strip. Fold each strip like a flag, in triangles. Brush with butter. Repeat the process until all the ingredients are used. May be frozen at this point. Bake at 375 degrees for 20 minutes or for 25 to 30 minutes if frozen.

Yield: 80 triangles

CONFEDERATE SAUSAGE BALLS WITH JEZEBEL SAUCE

1 pound bulk sage sausage
8 ounces extra-sharp Cheddar
cheese, shredded

2 cups baking mix
Jezebel Sauce

Combine the sausage and cheese in a bowl and mix well. Knead in the baking mix. Shape into small balls. May be frozen at this point. Bake at 350 degrees for 20 to 25 minutes or until cooked through. Serve with Jezebel Sauce.

Yield: 70 balls

JEZEBEL SAUCE

1 (10-ounce) jar pineapple
preserves
1 (10-ounce) jar apple jelly
1 (5-ounce) jar horseradish

$1/2$ ($1^1/2$-ounce) can dry
mustard
1 teaspoon pepper

Combine the preserves, jelly, horseradish, mustard and pepper in a bowl and mix well.

ELEGANT EGGNOG

Mr. Low's eggnog recipe has been handed down for generations in the South. It is typical of what Andrew Low in the 1850s might have supervised being prepared by his butler, Tom Milledge, before a gala party at the Lows' elegant house on LaFayette Square. This eggnog is very rich and delicious. For a smaller party, cut the recipe in half.

Before preparing, have the big silver punch bowl and cups polished. Do likewise to the tray and ladle. Beat 12 egg yolks until very light. Add 2 cups sugar and beat again. Slowly add 1 quart French brandy and 1 pint Jamaican rum, beating constantly. Beat 12 egg whites very stiff, then fold $3/4$ of egg whites into mixture. Whip $1^1/2$ quarts heavy cream until very stiff and gently fold cream into mixture. Pour mixture into punch bowl and decorate top with reserved egg whites. Generously grate nutmeg over all.

Broughton Street Scallops

3 tablespoons unsalted butter
1 pound bay scallops,
cut into quarters
2 teaspoons lemon zest
3 garlic cloves, minced
3 teaspoons chopped
fresh dillweed

2 cups shredded Swiss cheese
2¼ cups mayonnaise
Pepper to taste
12 dozen (1-inch) white bread
rounds
Paprika to taste

Melt the butter in a skillet. Add the scallops, lemon zest and garlic. Cook for 2 to 3 minutes. Stir in the dill. Remove from heat and cool to room temperature. Add the cheese, mayonnaise and pepper and mix well. Lightly toast the bread rounds. Preheat the broiler. Top each round with a heaping teaspoon of the scallop mixture. Sprinkle with paprika. Broil 5 inches from the heat source for 2 to 3 minutes or until golden brown. Garnish with dill sprigs.

Yield: 144 scallop toasts

Pickled Shrimp

5 pounds shrimp, cooked,
peeled
½ cup sugar
2½ tablespoons paprika
3½ teaspoons salt
2½ cups olive oil
½ cup tarragon vinegar
½ cup catsup

Juice of 4½ lemons
2½ tablespoons steak sauce
Tabasco sauce to taste
1¼ teaspoons dry mustard
4 (4-ounce) jars button
mushrooms, drained
1 medium Vidalia onion,
thinly sliced

Place the shrimp in a large nonreactive pan. Combine the sugar, paprika, salt, olive oil, vinegar, catsup, lemon juice, steak sauce, Tabasco sauce, mustard, mushrooms and onion in a bowl and mix well. Pour over the shrimp. Refrigerate, covered, for 8 hours or for several days, turning often; drain. Arrange on a serving platter. Serve with wheat thin crackers.

Yield: 15 to 20 servings

GEORGIA BOILED PEANUTS

2 cups raw peanuts   1 tablespoon salt

Rinse peanuts thoroughly in cool water. Soak in cool water in a bowl for 30 minutes; drain. Combine the peanuts with enough water to cover in a saucepan. Add the salt. Bring to a boil. Reduce the heat. Simmer for 35 minutes or until peanuts are tender. Add additional salt if desired. Drain. Let stand until dry. Store in airtight containers. May be frozen.

Yield: 4 servings

SOUTHERN GLAZED PECANS

These are time consuming but worth the effort. The chile peppers give the pecans a flavor different from the usual sugared nuts.

$^1/_2$ cup water   1 cup pecans
$^1/_2$ cup sugar $^1/_4$ cup molasses
2 dried red chile peppers

Combine the water, sugar and peppers in a saucepan. Bring to a boil over high heat. Add the pecans and return to a boil. Reduce the heat. Simmer for 10 minutes; drain. Arrange the pecans evenly on a baking sheet. Bake at 250 degrees for 45 minutes; cool. Combine the cooled pecans and molasses in a bowl. Toss to coat. Arrange the pecans evenly on a greased baking sheet. Bake for 45 minutes or until crisp.

Yield: 3 servings

As every true southerner knows, peanuts grow underground. They are a member of the legume family. In late August and on into September, growers will be busy plowing up their crop, shaking the dirt from the nuts with machines, and separating the kernels from the vines with a peanut combine.

Back Porch Lime Daiquiris

2 (6-ounce) cans frozen
limeade concentrate, thawed
1 (6-ounce) can frozen
lemonade concentrate, thawed
4^1/$_2$ cups rum

4^1/$_2$ cups water
1 teaspoon sweetened lime juice
Lime slices
Maraschino cherries

Combine the limeade concentrate, lemonade concentrate, rum, water and lime juice in a freezer container and mix well. Freeze, covered, for 8 hours or longer. Place 3 to 4 cups in a blender container. Process until smooth. Serve in glasses with lime slices and cherries.

Yield: 12 servings

Yacht Club Sangria

1 part orange juice, chilled
1 part vegetable juice
cocktail, chilled

Squeeze of lime
Tabasco sauce to taste

Combine the orange juice, vegetable juice cocktail, lime juice and Tabasco sauce in a bowl and mix well. Serve in a glass with a shot of tequila on the side to sip.

Yield: Variable

One debutante of more than 45 years ago remembers when punch without the "spike" was customarily at tea dances, although champagne was sometimes served at the elaborate parties. A lavish supper night consists of ham, turkey, duck, venison, baked terrapin, salads, cakes, charlottes, coffee and champagne.

"The Age of Pavilions," Cliff Sewell. 10.4.64, *Savannah Morning News*

FROM
PEACH FRITTERS
TO
QUICHE

BREADS AND BREAKFAST

THE
OWENS-THOMAS
HOUSE

THE MARQUIS DE LAFAYETTE

In 1825, on the eve of the fiftieth anniversary of the signing of the
Declaration of Independence, the French nobleman who had volunteered
to assist the American colonists in their fight for freedom returned to
the United States for an extended triumphal tour. City leaders prevailed
upon LaFayette to visit Savannah to lay the cornerstones to monuments
for Revolutionary war heroes General Nathaniel Green and Count

Casimir Pulaski. He arrived in March, staying at the grand mansion that architect John Jay had built for banker Richard Richardson (now known as the Owens-Thomas House of the Telfair Museum of Art).

After the cornerstones were laid, a celebratory dinner was held in LaFayette's honor at the city hall. The event was held in the Council Chamber, which, according to an official account of the visit, "was prepared for the occasion with arches, branches, etc...." The dinner was comprised of "a profusion of substantial fare, and every delicacy of the season. The Company including the guests, were at least three hundred in number." As was common in the nineteenth century, there were a series of official toasts. At this event there were thirteen. Then followed thirty-eight "volunteer toasts." The elderly general retired for the evening after the eighteenth volunteer toast. He missed the performance of a song that had been specially composed in his honor for the occasion.

"... a celebratory dinner was held in LaFayette's honor at the city hall."

An Account of the Reception of Gen. LaFayette in Savannah on Saturday, March 19th, 1825. Savannah, Georgia: W. T. Williams, 1825.

COMPANY QUICHE

Great for breakfast, brunch, lunch, or dinner.

1 (9-inch) deep-dish pie shell
$^1/_2$ cup chopped ham
12 ounces bacon, cooked, crumbled
$^3/_4$ cup cooked chopped link sausage

$^3/_4$ cup shredded sharp cheese
1 cup sour cream
2 eggs, beaten

Preheat oven to 350 degrees. Bake the pie shell for 10 minutes or until browned. Layer the ham, $^1/_4$ cup of the cheese, bacon, $^1/_4$ cup of the cheese and the sausage in the pie shell. Combine the sour cream and eggs in a bowl and mix well. Spoon over the layers. Sprinkle the remaining $^1/_4$ cup cheese over the top. Bake for 1 hour, covering with foil after 45 minutes.

Yield: 6 servings

SAPELO BRUNCH EGGS

1 beef or chicken bouillon cube
1 tablespoon hot water
1 pound mushrooms, sliced
$^1/_4$ cup butter
3 tablespoons flour
1 tablespoon grated onion

2 cups heavy cream
1 egg yolk, beaten
Salt and pepper to taste
6 to 8 eggs
Grated Parmesan cheese to taste
1 tablespoon chopped parsley

Preheat oven to 350 degrees. Dissolve the bouillon in hot water in a cup. Sauté the mushrooms in butter in a skillet. Add the dissolved bouillon, flour and onion and mix well. Cook until mixture thickens. Stir in the cream slowly. Stir a small amount of the hot mixture into the beaten egg yolk. Stir the egg yolk into the hot mixture. Pour into a baking dish. Crack the eggs over the mixture, 1 at a time. Sprinkle with Parmesan cheese and parsley. Bake for 15 minutes or until eggs are set.

Yield: 6 to 8 servings

LIBERTY BOYS CHEESE STRATA

This recipe was passed down in my family by my mother.

14 slices bread, trimmed
Butter to taste, softened
Mustard to taste
2 cups shredded sharp Cheddar cheese
$2^1/_2$ cups milk
4 eggs
1 teaspoon salt
1 teaspoon pepper
$^1/_2$ teaspoon paprika
$^1/_2$ teaspoon cayenne
10 to 12 slices bacon

Spread 7 slices of bread with butter. Spread 7 slices of bread with mustard. Arrange 7 bread slices over the bottom of an 8x12-inch baking dish, alternating the butter and mustard slices. Sprinkle 1 cup of the cheese over the bread slices. Repeat with remaining bread slices and cheese. Combine the milk, eggs, salt, pepper, paprika and cayenne in a bowl and mix well. Pour over the layers. Arrange the bacon strips over the top. Refrigerate, covered, for 8 to 12 hours. Preheat oven to 375 degrees. Place the baking dish in a larger baking pan and add enough hot water to reach halfway up the sides. Bake for 60 to 65 minutes. Let stand for 2 minutes before serving.

Yield: 10 servings

For two centuries, Savannah's cuisine was a secret, not by intent but because the cooks who presided over the kitchen were artists who could never communicate the ingredients and procedures of their culinary masterpieces.

"Cookin' lak religion is/some elected an' some ain't an' rules don' no mo mek a cook/den sermons make a saint," As Mrs. Colquitt's cook used to say.

Betsy Fancher—Book, *Savannah: A Renaissance of the Heart*

SUNBURY EGG CASSEROLE

8 hard-cooked eggs
$1/4$ cup melted margarine
$1/2$ teaspoon Worcestershire sauce
$1/4$ teaspoon prepared mustard
1 teaspoon chopped parsley
1 teaspoon chopped chives
$1/2$ cup finely chopped ham

1 tablespoon mayonnaise
3 tablespoons butter
3 tablespoons flour
1 cup chicken broth
$3/4$ cup milk
6 chopped green olives
Dash of salt and pepper
1 cup shredded Cheddar cheese

Peel the eggs. Cut into halves lengthwise. Mash the yolks in a bowl. Add the magarine, Worcestershire sauce, mustard, parsley, chives, ham and mayonnaise and mix well. Spoon into the egg whites. Place filled egg whites in a greased 9x13-inch baking dish. Melt the butter in a saucepan. Stir in the flour. Cook for 2 minutes, stirring constantly. Add the broth and milk, whisking constantly. Bring to a simmer. Simmer until smooth and thickened. Stir in the olives, salt and pepper. Pour over the eggs. Sprinkle with the cheese. Bake at 350 degrees for 20 minutes.

Yield: 6 to 8 servings

CLASSIC SOUTHERN BREAKFAST SHRIMP

1 pound fresh medium shrimp
2 tablespoons lemon juice
$1/4$ teaspoon salt
$1/8$ teaspoon ground red pepper
$1/4$ cup finely chopped onion

$1/3$ cup finely chopped green bell pepper
3 tablespoons bacon drippings
2 tablespoons flour
$3/4$ cup shrimp stock or chicken broth

Peel and devein the shrimp. Combine the shrimp, lemon juice, salt and red pepper in a bowl and mix well. Cook the onion and bell pepper in the bacon drippings in a skillet over medium-high heat for 10 minutes or until tender, stirring constantly. Sprinkle with the flour. Cook for 2 minutes or until flour begins to brown, stirring constantly. Add the shrimp mixture and shrimp stock. Cook for 2 to 3 minutes or until shrimp turn pink, stirring constantly. Add water or additional stock if sauce is too thick. Serve over creamy grits.

Yield: 4 servings

CHILE CHEESE BREAD

Bake in miniature loaf pans and give as gifts!

4 cups baking mix
2 cups shredded Colby,
Monterey Jack or Cheddar cheese
1 1/2 cups milk
2 eggs, beaten

1/4 cup margarine
1 (4-ounce) can chopped green chiles, drained
1/4 teaspoon ground red pepper
Hot peppers to taste (optional)

Combine the baking mix and cheese in a bowl and mix well. Combine the milk, eggs, margarine, green chiles, red pepper and hot peppers in a separate bowl and mix well. Add the dry ingredients and stir just until mixed. Pour into a greased 5x9-inch loaf pan. Place loaf pan on a baking sheet. Bake for 55 minutes or until loaf tests done. Cool in the pan for 10 minutes. Remove to a wire rack to cool completely.

Yield: 12 slices

MULBERRY GROVE CHEESE BREAD

This bread was served at a luncheon and was the inspiration for a benefit cookbook for the Los Angeles Child Advocates program.

1 egg
1/4 cup milk
1/8 teaspoon salt
12 slices white bread

3/4 cup butter, melted
1 1/2 cups grated Parmesan cheese

Beat the egg, milk and salt in a mixer bowl. Trim the crusts from the bread. Dip 4 slices of bread in the egg mixture. Place each dipped slice between 2 of the remaining slices. Cut into 6 triangles. Dip each triangle in the melted butter. Roll in the Parmesan cheese to coat. Place triangles in a 10x15-inch baking pan. Bake at 375 degrees for 10 minutes or until lightly browned.

Yield: 6 servings

SPICY RICE CORN BREAD

This recipe is always a hit at family get-togethers and goes well with vegetable soup. You can vary the amount of hot sauce or omit it completely to suit your own taste!

1 cup yellow cornmeal
1 teaspoon salt
1 teaspoon pepper
1/2 teaspoon cayenne (optional)
1/2 teaspoon baking soda
1 cup milk
2 eggs or equivalent egg substitute, beaten
1/2 cup canola oil
1 (16-ounce) can cream-style corn
2 cups cooked white rice
1/2 cup finely chopped onion
1/4 cup thinly sliced green onions
1/4 cup finely chopped orange or red bell pepper
3 tablespoons peach hot sauce, or to taste
8 ounces Monterey Jack or Colby cheese, shredded

Coat a 12-inch square deep-dish baking pan with nonstick cooking spray. Sprinkle with a small amount of cornmeal. Combine the cornmeal, salt, pepper, cayenne and baking soda in a bowl and mix well. Combine the milk, eggs, oil, corn, rice, onion, green onions, orange pepper, hot sauce and cheese in a separate bowl and mix well. Add to the dry ingredients, stirring just until mixed. Spoon into the prepared pan. Sprinkle with additional cheese and paprika if desired. Bake at 350 degrees for 45 minutes.

Yield: 24 servings

"One of the calls is used by the seller of honey, an aged, decrepit Negro who walks through the streets with his basket balanced on his head, calling in monotonous tones as he walks: 'Here comes the honey man—I gets honey in de comb—yes, ma'am, I gots honey cheap—here comes the honey man.'"
Excerpt from article in *Savannah News*, "Street Calls of the South"

Pineapple Cheese Braid

2 envelopes active dry yeast
1 cup warm (110- to 115-degree) water
$^1/_2$ cup butter or margarine, softened
5 tablespoons sugar
2 eggs
$^1/_4$ teaspoon salt
$4^1/_4$ to $4^1/_2$ cups flour
Cream Cheese Filling
Pineapple Filling
1 cup confectioners' sugar
2 to 3 tablespoons milk

Dissolve the yeast in warm water in a mixer bowl. Let stand for 5 minutes. Add the butter, sugar, eggs, salt and 2 cups of the flour. Beat at low speed for 3 minutes. Add enough of the remaining flour to form a soft dough. Knead on a floured surface for 6 to 8 minutes or until smooth and elastic. Place in a greased bowl, turning to coat the surface. Let rise, covered, in a warm place for 45 minutes or until doubled in bulk. Punch the dough down. Divide into 2 portions. Roll each portion into a 9x15-inch rectangle. Place on greased baking sheets. Spread half of the Cream Cheese Filling lengthwise down the center third of each rectangle. Spread half of the Pineapple Filling over the cream cheese. Cut 1-inch-wide strips on each side 3 inches into the center. Fold alternating strips at an angle across the filling, starting at one end. Seal the ends. Let rise for 20 minutes or until doubled in bulk. Bake at 350 degrees for 25 to 30 minutes or until golden brown. Cool on a wire rack. Combine the confectioners' sugar and enough milk to make of a spreading consistency in a bowl and mix well. Drizzle over the bread.

Yield: 24 slices

Cream Cheese Filling

16 ounces cream cheese, softened
$^1/_3$ cup sugar
1 tablespoon lemon juice
$^1/_2$ teaspoon vanilla extract

Combine the cream cheese, sugar, lemon juice and vanilla in a mixer bowl. Beat until smooth.

Pineapple Filling

1 (8-ounce) can crushed pineapple
$^1/_2$ cup sugar
3 tablespoons cornstarch

Combine the pineapple, sugar and cornstarch in a saucepan and mix well. Bring to a boil. Reduce the heat. Cook until thickened, stirring constantly.

Raisin Granola Bread

2 envelopes active dry yeast
2 cups warm (105- to 115-degree) water
1 cup warm (105- to 115-degree) milk
2 teaspoons salt
$^{1}/_{2}$ cup vegetable oil
$^{1}/_{3}$ cup honey
8 to 9 cups bread flour
$^{1}/_{2}$ cup granola
$^{1}/_{2}$ cup sunflower kernels
$^{1}/_{2}$ cup raisins
2 tablespoons grated orange peel
1 egg
1 tablespoon milk

Dissolve the yeast in the warm water and warm milk in a mixer bowl. Add the salt, oil and honey and mix well. Beat in 4 cups of the flour at low speed until moistened. Beat at medium speed for 3 minutes. Stir in the granola, sunflower kernels, raisins and orange peel. Stir in enough of the remaining flour to make a soft dough. Knead in the remaining flour on a floured surface for 10 minutes or until dough is smooth and elastic. Place in a greased bowl, turning to coat the surface. Let rise, covered, in a warm place for 1 hour or until doubled in bulk. Punch the dough down several times to remove air bubbles. Let rise for 15 minutes. Divide into 3 portions. Shape each into a loaf and place in a greased 4x8-inch loaf pan. Let rise, covered, in a warm place for 45 to 60 minutes or until doubled in bulk. Preheat oven to 350 degrees. Combine the egg and 1 tablespoon milk in a bowl and mix well. Brush over the top of each loaf. Bake for 35 to 45 minutes or until deep golden brown and loaves sound hollow when lightly tapped. Remove from the pans immediately. Cool on a wire rack.

Yield: 36 slices

It's grist before it is cooked and hominy afterwards...
So wash your grist in several waters, cover it in the preparation of one part grist and three
parts of water and put it on the stove in a double boiler with salt to taste. Let it boil
for one hour or more, stirring frequently to keep from any lumping.

Betsy Fancher—Book, *Savannah: A Renaissance of the Heart*

STRAWBERRY NUT BREAD

3 cups flour	3 eggs, well beaten
1 teaspoon baking soda	1 1/4 cups vegetable oil
1 teaspoon salt	2 (10-ounce) packages frozen
1 tablespoon cinnamon	strawberries, thawed
2 cups sugar	1 1/4 cups nuts

Combine the flour, baking soda, salt, cinnamon and sugar in a bowl and mix well. Beat the eggs with the oil in a mixer bowl. Add to the dry ingredients and mix well. Stir in the strawberries and nuts. Spoon into 2 large or 3 small greased and floured loaf pans. Bake at 350 degrees for 1 hour or until golden brown. Cool in the pans for 10 minutes. Remove to a wire rack to cool completely. Serve with cream cheese.

Yield: 24 servings

ZUCCHINI FLOWERPOT BREAD

1 cup all-purpose flour	1/4 teaspoon ground cloves
1/2 cup whole wheat flour	1 egg
1/2 cup sugar	1 egg white
1 teaspoon baking powder	3 tablespoons vegetable oil
1/2 teaspoon baking soda	1 medium zucchini, grated
1/4 teaspoon cinnamon	1 teaspoon vanilla extract
1/4 teaspoon nutmeg	1/2 cup crushed pineapple, drained

Wash and dry 8 new 2 1/2- to 3-inch-diameter flowerpots. Spray the insides with nonstick cooking spray. Preheat oven to 350 degrees. Combine the all-purpose flour, whole wheat flour, sugar, baking powder, baking soda, cinnamon, nutmeg and cloves in a bowl and mix well. Combine the egg, egg white, oil, zucchini, vanilla and pineapple in a separate bowl and mix well. Add the dry ingredients and stir just until moistened. Pour evenly into the flowerpots. Bake for 35 to 40 minutes or until a wooden pick inserted in the center comes out clean and top is browned.

Yield: 8 servings

MELT-IN-YOUR-MOUTH BEER MUFFINS

3 cups baking mix   1 (12-ounce) can beer
3 tablespoons sugar

Combine the baking mix, sugar and beer in a bowl and mix well. Let stand for 15 minutes. Fill greased muffin cups ²/₃ full. Bake at 350 degrees for 10 to 15 minutes or until lightly browned on top. Serve warm.

Yield: 18 muffins

BRAN MUFFINS

1 (15-ounce) package   2 teaspoons salt
Raisin Bran   4 eggs, beaten
3 cups sugar   1 cup vegetable oil
5 cups flour   4 cups buttermilk
4 to 5 teaspoons baking soda

Combine the Raisin Bran, sugar, flour, baking soda and salt in a bowl and mix well. Combine the eggs, oil and buttermilk in a separate bowl and mix well. Pour into the dry ingredients and stir just until mixed. Fill greased muffin cups ²/₃ full. Bake at 400 degrees for 15 minutes. Cool in the pan for 10 minutes. Remove to a wire rack to cool completely. May store batter, covered, for 4 to 5 weeks in the refrigerator.

Yield: 30 muffins

Relief from the summer heat first came to Savannah in 1818 when ice was imported. It was advertised at 6¹/₄ cents per pound and touted as "highly desirable to cool water, milk and wine."

Page 56, Excerpt from Edward Chang Sieg, *Eden on the Marsh: An Illustrated History of Savannah*, 1985. Windsor Publications.

SPICY OATMEAL MUFFINS

1¹/₂ cups boiling water
1 cup quick-cooking oats
¹/₂ cup margarine or applesauce
1¹/₂ cups packed brown sugar
¹/₂ cup sugar

2 eggs
1¹/₂ cups flour
1 teaspoon salt
1 teaspoon baking soda
¹/₂ teaspoon cinnamon

Pour the boiling water over the oats and margarine in a bowl. Let stand for 20 minutes. Cream the brown sugar, sugar and eggs in a mixer bowl. Stir in the oatmeal mixture. Add the flour, salt, baking soda and cinnamon and mix well. Fill greased and floured muffin cups ²/₃ full. Bake at 350 degrees for 25 minutes. Cool in the pan for 10 minutes. Remove to a wire rack to cool completely.

Yield: 18 muffins

PEACH MUFFINS

2 cups plus 2 tablespoons flour
¹/₂ cup sugar
2 teaspoons baking powder
¹/₂ teaspoon baking soda
¹/₂ teaspoon salt
1 teaspoon cinnamon
¹/₂ teaspoon nutmeg
Dash of mace
1 egg, lightly beaten

¹/₃ cup vegetable oil
¹/₃ cup milk
1 (8-ounce) carton peach yogurt
¹/₂ cup finely chopped dried peaches
2 tablespoons brown sugar
2 tablespoons chopped pecans
2 tablespoons margarine, softened

Preheat oven to 400 degrees. Combine 2 cups of the flour, sugar, baking powder, baking soda, salt, ¹/₂ teaspoon of the cinnamon, nutmeg and mace in a bowl and mix well. Make a well in the center. Combine the egg, oil, milk, yogurt and dried peaches in a separate bowl and mix well. Add to the dry ingredients and stir just until mixed. Fill greased muffin cups ²/₃ full. Combine the remaining 2 tablespoons flour, brown sugar, pecans and remaining ¹/₂ teaspoon cinnamon in a bowl and mix well. Cut in the margarine until crumbly. Sprinkle 1 heaping teaspoonful over batter in each muffin cup. Bake for 20 minutes or until golden brown. Cool in the pan for 10 minutes. Serve warm or at room temperature.

Yield: 18 muffins

GEORGIA PEACH FRITTERS

2 cups flour, sifted
1 tablespoon baking powder
$1/2$ teaspoon salt
$1/3$ cup butter
$1/2$ cup sugar

$1/2$ teaspoon vanilla extract
2 eggs, beaten
$3/4$ cup milk
$1^1/2$ cups chopped peaches
$1/2$ teaspoon lemon juice

Sift the flour, baking powder and salt together. Cream the butter, sugar and vanilla in a mixer bowl until light and fluffy. Beat in the eggs. Beat in the dry ingredients alternately with the milk. Combine the peaches and lemon juice in a bowl and mix well. Fold into the batter. Drop by teaspoonfuls into deep 365-degree oil. Deep-fry for 3 to 4 minutes or until golden brown, turning once. Drain on paper towels. Serve with whipped cream or sprinkle with confectioners' sugar.

Yield: 4 dozen

SOUTHERN SCONES

$1/2$ cup golden raisins
$1/2$ cup bourbon
$1/2$ cup cold butter, chopped into small pieces
$2^1/2$ cups self-rising flour, sifted
3 tablespoons sugar

1 egg
$2/3$ cup half-and-half
$1/2$ cup butter, melted
Clotted cream
Orange marmalade

Preheat oven to 425 degrees. Combine the raisins and bourbon in a saucepan. Bring to a simmer. Simmer until raisins are tender and plump; drain. Cut the butter into the flour in a bowl until crumbly. Stir in the sugar and raisins. Combine the egg and half-and-half in a separate bowl and mix well. Add to the flour mixture and stir until mixture forms a ball. Knead on a lightly floured surface 4 or 5 times. Roll into a small circle and fold over. Roll 1 inch thick. Cut into circles. Place on a buttered baking sheet. Bake for 12 minutes or until light brown. May be frozen at this point and reheated on an ungreased baking sheet at 425 degrees for 10 minutes. Brush with melted butter. Serve with clotted cream and orange marmalade. If clotted cream is unavailable substitute a mixture of $1/2$ cup cream cheese, $1/4$ cup sour cream and $1/4$ cup heavy cream.

Yield: 1 dozen

MARGIE'S ROLLS

1 envelope active dry yeast	$1/2$ cup cold milk or ice water
$1/4$ cup warm water	$3 1/2$ cups flour
$1/2$ cup boiling water	1 teaspoon salt
$1/4$ cup shortening	1 egg
$1/4$ cup margarine or butter	2 tablespoons melted butter
$1/4$ cup (scant) sugar	

Dissolve the yeast in the warm water in a bowl. Pour the boiling water over the shortening and margarine in a separate bowl and stir until shortening and margarine are melted. Stir in the sugar. Stir in the milk. Add 2 cups of the flour and the salt and mix until almost smooth. Add the egg and dissolved yeast and mix well. Stir in the remaining $1 1/2$ cups flour. May refrigerate dough, covered, overnight. Roll $1/2$ inch thick on a lightly floured surface. Cut with a biscuit cutter and fold. Place on a baking sheet covered with foil. Brush with melted butter. May let rise for 3 to 4 hours. Bake at 400 degrees for 15 minutes or until browned.

Yield: 8 servings

NICE AND EASY DINNER ROLLS

1 (10-count) can refrigerator biscuits	1 cup caraway, sesame or poppy seeds
1 cup whole milk	

Cut each biscuit into 4 pieces. Shape each piece into a ball. Dip into the milk. Roll in the seeds to coat. Bake using package directions. Serve immediately.

Yield: 40 biscuits

In the 3 years from the fall of Fort Pulaski to the coming of Sherman,
Savannah gradually starved.
Page 68, Excerpt from Edward Chang Sieg, *Eden on the Marsh: An Illustrated History of Savannah*, 1985. Windsor Publications.

CRANBERRY COFFEE CAKE

2 cups sifted flour
1 tablespoon baking powder
$^3/4$ teaspoon salt
1 cup sugar
$^1/2$ cup butter

1 egg, beaten
$^1/2$ cup milk
$2^1/2$ cups fresh cranberries, coarsely chopped
$^1/4$ cup flour

Sift the sifted flour, baking powder, salt and $^1/2$ cup of the sugar into a bowl. Cut in 5 tablespoons of the butter until crumbly. Combine the egg and milk in a separate bowl and mix well. Add gradually to the flour mixture, beating until well blended. Spread evenly in a buttered 8-inch square baking pan. Sprinkle with cranberries. Combine the flour and remaining $^1/2$ cup sugar in a bowl and mix well. Cut in the remaining 3 tablespoons butter until crumbly. Sprinkle over the cranberries. Bake at 375 degrees for 30 to 35 minutes. Cut into 9 squares.

Yield: 9 servings

IRISH FESTIVAL FUNNEL CAKES

3 cups flour
$^1/4$ cup sugar
1 tablespoon baking powder
$^1/4$ teaspoon salt
2 eggs

1 cup milk
1 cup water
$^1/2$ teaspoon vanilla extract
Vegetable oil

Combine the flour, sugar, baking powder and salt in a bowl and mix well. Beat the eggs in a mixer bowl until pale yellow. Beat in the milk, water and vanilla. Add the flour mixture, beating until smooth. Heat oil in an electric skillet or deep fryer to 375 degrees. Ladle $^1/2$ cup of batter into a funnel, holding your finger over the spout. Hold the funnel several inches above the skillet, release the spout and move the funnel in a spiral motion until all the batter is released. Fry for 2 minutes on each side or until golden brown. Drain on paper towels. Sprinkle with confectioners' sugar. Serve warm.

Yield: 8 cakes

ORANGE COFFEE CAKE

1 cup sour cream
1 (6-ounce) can frozen orange juice concentrate, thawed
4 eggs
1 (2-layer) package yellow cake mix

Combine the sour cream, orange juice concentrate, eggs and cake mix in a mixer bowl. Beat for 4 minutes or until smooth and creamy. Pour into a greased bundt pan. Bake at 350 degrees for 50 to 60 minutes or until cake tests done. Cool in the pan for 10 minutes. Invert onto a serving plate. Drizzle with an orange marmalade confectioners' sugar icing if desired.

Yield: 16 servings

Cane Grinding Time

For the old farm mule, it's just another job of work, tramping a never ending circle hitched to the pole which turns the mill. But for the herds of porkers, if they are lucky, it means varying degrees of inebriation, according to the amount of "buck" (fermented cane skimming) they can salvage from overturned barrels.

As for the syrup, tastes vary as to the proper degree of thickness, the exact color and clarity of the finished product as it comes from the old-fashioned iron kettles or the more modern evaporator.

Farmers vie with each other as to the quality of their respective products, but all are agreed good syrup bottled in colorless, transparent bottles, will bring a higher price on the market than syrup packed in metal.

While the sandwiches are being served, and the hosts cigars are lighted there are those who declare purple and striped, or pure ribbon cane are best because of their chewing qualities, while others insist the newly developed Cayanna No. 10, which is not so good for chewing but makes up for this deficit when it goes through the mill, is the best variety to grow.

And so the cane grinding goes on with Lowndes County syrup makers doing their annual stint towards producing some of the finest "Gawguh" cane to top the winter morning waffles in the city dwellers' homes.

Savannah Evening Press, "Cane Grinding Time South Georgia" (Wednesday, December 7, 1932)

COTTAGE CHEESE PANCAKES

1 cup cottage cheese
4 eggs, beaten
6 tablespoons margarine or butter, melted

$1/2$ cup flour
Pinch of salt
2 teaspoons sugar

Combine the cottage cheese, eggs, margarine, flour, salt and sugar in a bowl and mix well. Pour 2 tablespoons at a time onto a hot lightly buttered griddle. Bake for 2 to 3 minutes or until lightly browned on the underside. Turn pancake over. Bake until browned. Place on a heated platter.

Yield: 4 to 6 pancakes

UPTOWN WAFFLES

$3^1/2$ cups flour
4 teaspoons baking soda
1 teaspoon salt
2 tablespoons sugar

3 eggs
$3/4$ cup vegetable oil
3 cups milk

Combine the flour, baking soda, salt and sugar in a bowl and mix well. Combine the eggs, oil and milk in a separate bowl and mix well. Add the dry ingredients, stirring just until mixed. Bake in a waffle iron using manufacturer's instructions.

Yield: 4 large waffles

FROM

SHRIMP CHOWDER

TO

BLACKEYED PEA SALAD

SOUPS AND SALADS

THE
JULIETTE
GORDON LOW
HOUSE

TRUSTEES GARDEN

The ten-acre tract of land for the garden was cleared within one month of the colonists' settling on the bluff. The trustees were counting on the colony for the cultivation of commodities that England was importing at great expense, especially silk, olive oil, and wine.

The idea was to experiment with plants and herbs from all over the world to determine which ones might have an economic future in Georgia, given the climate and soil condition of the colony. Botanists were sent by the trustees to the West Indies and South America on plant-procuring forays. They brought back cuttings of flax, hemp, indigo, and cochineal olives. Medicinal herbs were also grown. Primary emphasis was on making silk production a success. In fact, of each fifty acres of land awarded to the colonists, ten were required to be planted with one hundred White Mulberry trees.

The first eight pounds of silk ever produced in the colony were sent to Queen Charlotte, who wove it into a dress she wore on her birthday.

Other crops had more potential. Experiments from this first economic garden in America deemed it feasible to produce the famed upland short staple cotton, which later comprised the greater portion of the world's cotton commerce. Here also, were propagated the peach trees that became so profitable in both Georgia and South Carolina.

"The first eight pounds of silk ever produced in the colony were sent to Queen Charlotte..."

...Savannah: People, Places and Events, Ron Freeman, 1998.

CREAM OF BROCCOLI SOUP

This is delicious either hot or cold. You can top each serving with a spoonful of low-fat sour cream and chopped chives, dill or parsley.

1 large onion, coarsely chopped
1 medium carrot, sliced
1 small celery rib with leaves, sliced
1 garlic clove, finely chopped
3 cups chicken stock

$^1/4$ cup rice
3 cups coarsely chopped broccoli
2 cups low-fat milk
1 teaspoon salt
Pinch of cayenne

Combine the onion, carrot, celery, garlic and chicken stock in a large saucepan. Bring to a boil. Add the rice. Simmer, covered, for 15 to 20 minutes or until the rice is tender. Add the broccoli. Simmer for 5 minutes or until the broccoli is tender. Purée in a blender. Return to the saucepan. Stir in the milk, salt and cayenne. Cook until heated through. Ladle into soup bowls.

Yield: 8 ($^3/4$-cup) servings

TRUSTEES CORN CHOWDER

8 ounces bacon, diced
1 medium onion, chopped
$^1/2$ cup chopped celery
2 tablespoons flour
4 cups milk
1 (17-ounce) can cream-style corn

1 (16-ounce) can tiny whole potatoes, chopped
$^1/2$ teaspoon salt
$^1/8$ teaspoon pepper
Homemade croutons (optional)

Cook the bacon in a skillet until crisp. Remove the bacon and pour off the drippings, reserving 3 tablespoons. Cook the onion and celery in the drippings in the skillet until the onion is tender. Remove from heat. Stir in the flour. Cook over low heat until the mixture is bubbly, stirring constantly. Add the milk gradually, stirring constantly. Bring to a boil. Boil for 1 minute, stirring constantly. Stir in the corn, potatoes, salt and pepper. Cook until heated through. Stir in the cooked bacon. Ladle into soup bowls. Garnish with parsley and paprika. Top with homemade croutons. *Variation:* May prepare in a slow cooker using 4 cups milk, 2 cups half-and-half, 1 pound bacon, three 17-ounce cans cream-style corn and two 16-ounce cans tiny whole potatoes.

Yield: 6 (1-cup) servings

BILL'S ONION SOUP

1 large onion, sliced	Salt and pepper to taste
1/4 cup butter	1 (49-ounce) can chicken broth
1/4 cup olive oil	6 slices French bread
1/4 cup premium whiskey	6 round slices provolone cheese

Sauté the onion in the butter and olive oil in a stockpot until transparent. Add the whiskey. Ignite with a match and let burn until the flame subsides. Stir in the salt, pepper and chicken stock. Bring to a simmer. Simmer for 45 minutes. Place a slice of French bread in the bottom of each of 6 oven-proof soup bowls. Ladle the soup over the bread; the bread will float to the top. Top each bread slice with a slice of cheese. Broil under a preheated broiler until the cheese melts. Serve immediately.

Yield: 6 servings

SQUASH BISQUE

1 large onion, chopped	4 cups yellow squash, sliced
1/2 cup butter or margarine	4 cups chicken broth
2 medium potatoes, peeled, chopped	1/4 teaspoon salt
	1/4 teaspoon ground red pepper
3 carrots, chopped	1 cup milk

Sauté the onion in the butter in a Dutch oven. Add the potatoes, carrots, squash, broth, salt and red pepper. Simmer, covered, for 1 hour, stirring occasionally. Purée in batches in a blender or food processor, scraping down the sides. Return to the Dutch oven. Stir in the milk. Bring to a boil. Reduce the heat. Cook until of serving temperature, stirring frequently. Garnish with sour cream and chopped fresh chives.

Yield: 12 (1-cup) servings

"With its distinctive Coastal cuisine, its legendary hospitality, pungent libations, and high hearted appreciation of the exquisite camaraderie of the table, Savannah has a tradition of fine dining and civilized drinking that dates back to the birth of the colony of Georgia."

Betsy Fancher, Former Senior Editor of *Atlanta Magazine*, Book, *Savannah: A Renaissance of the Heart*

HEARTY VEGETABLE SOUP

From Irving Victor, M.D.

1$^1/_2$ to 2 pounds chuck beef, cubed

1 large soup bone

2 tablespoons vegetable oil

3 large onions, quartered

4 ribs celery with leaves, cut into 2-inch pieces

4 large carrots, sliced into rounds

2 (20-ounce) cans whole tomatoes

1 large rutabaga, chopped

Salt and pepper to taste

Seasoned salt to taste

1 tablespoon sugar

6 cups water

3 bay leaves

2 (16-ounce) cans green peas

Kernels of 2 ears fresh corn

2 (20-ounce) cans whole kernel corn

1 pound fresh okra

1 pound lima or butter beans

Sear the beef cubes and soup bone in hot oil in a stockpot. Add the onions, celery, carrots, tomatoes, rutabaga, salt, pepper, seasoned salt and sugar. Add the water and stir to combine. Add the bay leaves, peas, corn, okra and beans. Stir to combine. Simmer for 1$^1/_2$ to 2 hours or until the vegetables are tender, adding water as needed. Season with salt and pepper. Remove the bay leaves.

Yield: 12 servings

Banquet in Honor of Admiral and Mrs. Dewey
By the City of Savannah/At the DeSoto Hotel/March 21, 1900
Blue Points, Haute Sauterne, Green Turtle Clear, Veno de Pasto, Olives, Small Patties,
Salted Almonds, Celery, Broiled Savannah Rockfish, Potatoes Duchesse, Tenderloin of Beef
mushrooms, Pontet canet, Sweetbreads, larded, Green Peas, Georgia Terrapin, ala DeSoto,
Maraschino Punch, Roasted Woodcock with cress, Cliquot Yellow Label Champagne, Lettuce and
Tomato Salad, Assorted Cakes, Roquefort Cheese, Fruits, Coffee, Charlotte Russe, Toasted
Crackers Crème de Menthe, Cigars, Cigarettes.
Excerpt from *Savannah News* article

Brunswick Stew

1 (3-pound) chicken
1 pound lean beef
1 pound lean pork
Salt and pepper to taste
3 medium onions, chopped
4 (16-ounce) cans tomatoes
5 tablespoons Worcestershire sauce
$1^1/2$ (14-ounce) bottles catsup
1 tablespoon Tabasco sauce
2 bay leaves
$^1/2$ (12-ounce) bottle chili sauce
$^1/2$ teaspoon dry mustard
$^1/4$ cup butter
3 tablespoons vinegar
2 (16-ounce) cans lima or butter beans
2 (16-ounce) cans cream-style corn
1 (15-ounce) can small green peas
3 small Irish potatoes, chopped (optional)
1 (10-ounce) package frozen sliced okra (optional)

Place the chicken, beef and pork in a large heavy pot. Season with salt and pepper. Add the onions. Cover with water. Simmer for several hours or until the meat falls from the bones. Remove from heat. Drain, reserving the stock. Shred the meat, discarding the bones. Combine the shredded meat and reserved stock in the pot. Add the tomatoes, Worcestershire sauce, catsup, Tabasco sauce, bay leaves, chili sauce, mustard and butter, stirring to combine. Cook for 1 hour, stirring occasionally. Add the vinegar, lima beans, corn, peas, potatoes and okra, stirring to combine. Cook over low heat until stew thickens.

Yield: 20 servings

RIVER STREET CHILI

A favorite cold-weather warm-up. Low-fat, tasty and a sure hit.

1 tablespoon olive oil
1 pound boneless skinless chicken breasts
1 medium onion, chopped
1 cup chicken broth
1 (4-ounce) can chopped green chiles
1 teaspoon minced garlic
$1/4$ teaspoon ground cumin
$1/2$ teaspoon oregano
$1/2$ teaspoon cilantro
$1/4$ teaspoon red pepper
1 (19-ounce) can Great Northern beans
Shredded low-fat Monterey Jack cheese

Heat the oil heat in a 3-quart saucepan over medium-high heat. Add the chicken. Cook for 5 to 6 minutes or until brown on both sides. Remove the chicken and cover to keep warm. Add the onion. Cook for 2 to 3 minutes. Stir in the broth, green chiles, garlic, cumin, oregano, cilantro and red pepper. Simmer for 30 minutes. Cut the chicken into cubes. Add the chicken and the undrained beans to the hot mixture. Simmer for 10 minutes. Garnish with Monterey Jack cheese.

Yield: 4 servings

To work up an appetite before dinner at Wild Heron, the oldest plantation in Savannah, soldiers were taken for a ride in an old wagon. Southern girls liked to hear the boys sing famous old 7th Regiment marching songs. Dinner at Wild Heron consisted of fried chicken, pilau (shrimp and rice), corn on the cob, lima beans, baked ham, ice cream and cake. Waitresses always wore the "old mammy" costumes.

CHICKEN JAMBALAYA

1/4 cup butter	2 bay leaves
1 cup chopped ham	1 teaspoon Cajun seasoning
3/4 cup chopped onion	1/2 teaspoon salt
2 tablespoons flour	2 cups instant rice
1 1/2 cups water	1 (15-ounce) package chicken tenders
1 (14-ounce) can stewed tomatoes	

Melt the butter in a 12-inch skillet over medium heat until sizzling. Add the ham and onion. Cook over medium heat for 5 to 7 minutes or until the onion is tender, stirring occasionally. Stir in the flour until blended. Add the water, tomatoes, bay leaves, Cajun seasoning and salt. Bring to a boil, stirring occasionally. Stir in the rice and chicken tenders. Cook, covered, for 10 to 15 minutes or until the rice is tender and the chicken is cooked through. Remove the bay leaf before serving.

Yield: 6 servings

SEAFOOD GUMBO

1 large onion, chopped	1 tablespoon Italian seasoning
1 large green bell pepper, chopped	1/4 teaspoon Tabasco sauce
2 ribs celery, chopped	8 ounces fresh fish of choice such as flounder, snapper or trout
2 tablespoons bacon drippings	1 pound shrimp, shelled, deveined
1 (32-ounce) can crushed tomatoes	1 pound crab meat
4 cups water	Salt and pepper to taste
1/4 cup Worcestershire sauce	

Sauté the onion, green pepper and celery in the bacon drippings in a skillet until the onion is tender. Stir in the tomatoes and water. Bring to a boil over medium heat. Reduce the heat. Simmer for 30 minutes. Stir in the Worcestershire sauce, Italian seasoning and Tabasco sauce. Cook for 10 minutes. Add the fish and shrimp. Cook for 10 minutes. Add the crab meat. Simmer for 20 minutes. Season with salt and pepper.

Yield: 6 servings

St. Catherine's Oyster Bisque

1 quart oysters
1 pint oysters (optional)
Salt and pepper to taste
4 ribs celery, chopped
1 medium onion, chopped
4 cups milk
2 cups whipping cream
1/4 cup butter
1/4 cup flour
Nutmeg to taste
Dash of curry powder
Dash of MSG
1 tablespoon lemon juice
1 tablespoon Worcestershire sauce
Red pepper to taste

Drain oysters and remove any shells. Combine oysters with salt and pepper in a saucepan. Simmer, covered, over low heat until the edges begin to curl, stirring occasionally. Drain the oysters, reserving the stock. Strain the stock into a bowl. Cook the celery and onion in water in a saucepan until tender. Drain, reserving the liquid. Pour the liquid into the oyster stock. Stir the milk and 1 3/4 cups of the whipping cream into the oyster stock. Heat the butter in a saucepan until melted. Stir in the flour. Add the milk mixture, whisking constantly. Cook until smooth and thickened, stirring constantly. Stir in the nutmeg, curry, MSG, lemon juice, Worcestershire sauce and red pepper. Adjust seasonings to taste. Grind the cooked oysters, onion and celery in a grinder. Keep warm over hot water until ready to serve. Whip the remaining 1/4 cup whipping cream in a mixer bowl. Combine the ground oyster mixture with the bisque and mix well. Ladle into soup bowls. Top with a dollop of whipped cream. Garnish with paprika and chopped parsley. Serve with sherry.

Yield: 6 (1-cup) servings

VIC'S SHRIMP CHOWDER

From Irving Victor, M.D.

1/2 cup butter	Salt and pepper to taste
2 ribs celery, chopped	1 (10-ounce) can chicken broth
2 large onions, chopped	
2 garlic cloves, minced	1 egg yolk
Shake & Sauce Thickener or flour	2 (11-ounce) cans white Shoe Peg corn
4 cups milk	Pinch of sugar, or to taste
8 ounces cream cheese, cut into pieces	2 (10-ounce) cans cream of potato soup
4 cups half-and-half	8 to 12 ounces shrimp, peeled

Melt the butter in a large saucepan. Add the celery, onions and garlic. Sauté over low heat until the onion is translucent. Stir in enough thickener to absorb the butter. Add the milk gradually, whisking constantly. Bring to a simmer. Simmer until thickened. Add the cream cheese, stirring until melted. Whisk in the half-and-half, salt and pepper. Whisk in the chicken broth and egg yolk. Stir in the corn, sugar and soup. Simmer for 30 minutes. Whisk in additional flour and simmer until of the desired consistency. Stir in the shrimp. Cook until the shrimp are pink; do not overcook. Ladle into bowls.

Yield: 12 to 14 servings

SECRET PARMESAN DRESSING

Combine 1 1/4 cups mayonnaise, 1 cup grated Parmesan cheese, 1/2 teaspoon salt, 1 teaspoon freshly ground pepper and 2 pressed garlic cloves in a bowl and mix well. Chill, covered, for 1 hour. Cut 1 head cauliflower into small pieces. Place in a food processor container. Pour in 1/4 cup water; purée. Drain the cauliflower. Stir into the mayonnaise mixture. Chill, covered, for 8 to 12 hours. Serve over mixed greens and vegetables.

Yield: 8 (1/4-cup) servings

ROMAINE SALAD WITH BLEU CHEESE, CHILI-TOASTED PECANS AND PEARS

¹/₂ cup sour cream

¹/₂ cup buttermilk

¹/₄ cup half-and-half

Juice of 1 orange

1 tablespoon minced fresh mint

2 teaspoons minced fresh basil

¹/₂ small shallot, minced

¹/₄ teaspoon salt

¹/₄ teaspoon cayenne

4 ounces bleu cheese, crumbled

2 ounces soft goat cheese, crumbled

Romaine lettuce, washed, torn into bite-size pieces, chilled

2 Bartlett pears, sliced lengthwise

3 to 4 tablespoons fresh lemon juice

Chili-Toasted Pecans

Peppercorns to taste

Combine the sour cream, buttermilk, half-and-half, orange juice, mint, basil, shallot, salt and cayenne in a bowl and mix well. Stir in the bleu cheese and goat cheese. Toss with the romaine lettuce in a bowl. Combine the pears and lemon juice in a bowl and toss to coat. Arrange the pears over the salad. Sprinkle with Chili-Toasted Pecans. Grind pepper over the top.

Yield: 4 to 6 servings

CHILI-TOASTED PECANS

1 cup pecan halves

2 tablespoons vegetable oil

2 teaspoons Kahlúa

1 tablespoon chili powder

¹/₄ teaspoon cayenne

2 teaspoons sugar

Preheat oven to 300 degrees. Toss the pecans with the oil and Kahlúa to coat in a bowl. Add the chili powder, cayenne and sugar and toss to coat. Spread on a baking sheet. Bake for 25 minutes or until toasted, stirring frequently. Cool.

SPINACH ORANGE SALAD

8 cups torn spinach leaves
2 (11-ounce) cans Mandarin
oranges, drained
1/2 cup sliced red onion

4 ounces feta cheese, crumbled
1/3 cup toasted sliced almonds
1 cup Oriental salad dressing

Combine the spinach, orange sections, onion, cheese and almonds in a large bowl. Toss to mix. Pour the salad dressing over the salad. Toss to coat. Serve immediately.

Yield: 6 to 8 servings

ZESTY CRANBERRY MOLD

2 (3-ounce) packages raspberry
gelatin
1/4 teaspoon salt
1/4 teaspoon cinnamon
Dash of cloves
2 cups boiling water

2 (8-ounce) cans whole
cranberry sauce
2 tablespoons grated orange peel
1 cup chopped orange sections
1 cup chopped apple

Combine the gelatin, salt, cinnamon and cloves in a bowl. Pour in the bowling water. Stir until the gelatin is dissolved. Add the cranberry sauce and orange peel and mix well. Chill until partially set. Fold in the oranges and apple. Pour into a mold. Chill until firm. Unmold onto a serving plate.

Yield: 8 servings

ORANGE NUT DRESSING

Beat 8 ounces softened cream cheese in a mixer bowl until light and fluffy. Add 1/4 cup orange juice concentrate, 1/2 teaspoon lemon juice, 2 tablespoons evaporated milk, 2 tablespoons sugar and a dash of salt. Beat until blended. Fold in 1/4 cup finely chopped pecans. Refrigerate until completely chilled.

Yield: 8 (1/4-cup) servings

ARTICHOKE SALAD

This salad is wonderful to make ahead and serve with ham.

1 (7-ounce) package chicken-flavor Rice-A-Roni

1 (6-ounce) jar marinated artichokes

1/3 cup mayonnaise

1/4 teaspoon curry

1 small bunch green onions, minced

1 (7-ounce) jar stuffed green olives, chopped

1 (8-ounce) can green peas, drained

Prepare the Rice-A-Roni using the package directions; cool. Combine with the artichokes, mayonnaise, curry, green onions, olives and peas in a bowl and mix well. Serve at room temperature.

Yield: 6 servings

BLACKEYED PEA SALAD

1 garlic clove, minced

1/4 cup rice vinegar

3 tablespoons extra-virgin olive oil

2 tablespoons orange juice

1/4 teaspoon Dijon mustard

Salt and pepper to taste

2 green onions, sliced

2 (15-ounce) cans blackeyed peas, drained, rinsed

1 small red bell pepper, chopped

1 rib celery, chopped

1 jicama, peeled, chopped

1 carrot, peeled, chopped

1/2 bunch fresh cilantro, finely chopped

Combine the garlic, vinegar, oil, juice, mustard, salt and pepper in a bowl and mix well. Add the remaining ingredients and stir to combine. Refrigerate, covered, for 8 to 10 hours. Serve cold.

Yield: 6 to 8 servings

WINE JELLY WITH FRUITS

Soften 2 tablespoons unflavored gelatin in 1/2 cup cold water in a bowl. Pour in 1 1/2 cups boiling water, stirring to dissolve the gelatin. Stir in 1 cup sugar, 1 cup sherry, 1/3 cup orange juice and 3 tablespoons lemon juice. Strain into a mold. Chill, covered, until firm. Unmold on a serving platter. Arrange fruits around the edge.

Yield: 24 (2-tablespoon) servings

PATTY'S BLACKEYED PEA SALAD

2 (15-ounce) cans blackeyed peas
with snaps, drained
$^{1}/_{2}$ cup thinly sliced red onion,
separated into rings
$^{1}/_{2}$ cup chopped green
bell pepper
1 small garlic clove

$^{1}/_{4}$ cup sugar
$^{1}/_{4}$ cup vinegar
$^{1}/_{4}$ cup vegetable oil
$^{1}/_{2}$ teaspoon salt
Dash of pepper
Dash of hot sauce

Combine the blackeyed peas, onion, green pepper and garlic in a bowl and mix well. Combine the sugar, vinegar, oil, salt, pepper and hot sauce in a separate bowl and mix well. Pour over the blackeyed pea mixture and toss to coat. Refrigerate, covered, for 12 hours or longer. Remove the garlic clove. Serve cold.

Yield: 6 to 8 servings

CAROLINA CABBAGE SALAD

From Chandler Echols, Chef
Savannah Golf Club

1 medium head cabbage,
finely shredded
2 large carrots, grated
1 cup chopped chives
1 red onion, sliced
1 white onion, sliced
1 cup olive oil

1 tablespoon crushed
black pepper
$^{1}/_{4}$ cup malt vinegar
$^{1}/_{4}$ cup raspberry vinegar
$^{1}/_{4}$ cup sugar
Salt to taste

Combine the cabbage and carrots in a bowl and mix well. Stir in the chives, red onion and white onion. Combine the oil, pepper, malt vinegar, raspberry vinegar, sugar and salt in a separate bowl and mix well. Pour over the cabbage mixture and mix well. Refrigerate for 1 hour before serving.

Yield: 6 servings

Marinated English Garden Salad

$^1/_3$ cup red wine vinegar
$^1/_3$ cup olive oil
$^3/_4$ teaspoon salt
$^1/_2$ teaspoon freshly ground pepper
3 garlic cloves, crushed
3 (15-ounce) cans English garden peas or black beans, rinsed, drained
1 (10-ounce) package frozen whole kernel corn, thawed
1 large red bell pepper, chopped
1 medium green bell pepper, chopped
1 purple onion, chopped

Combine the vinegar, oil, salt, pepper and garlic in a bowl and mix well. Let stand for 30 minutes. Combine the peas, corn, red pepper, green pepper and onion in a bowl and mix well. Pour the vinegar mixture over the pea mixture and toss to coat. Refrigerate, covered, for 8 hours. Garnish with chopped fresh parsley.

Yield: 10 to 12 servings

CURRY DIP

Combine $1^1/_2$ cups mayonnaise, 2 teaspoons curry powder, 1 tablespoon grated onion, $^1/_2$ teaspoon dry mustard, $^1/_2$ teaspoon salt, pepper to taste and a dash of Tabasco sauce in a bowl and mix well. Chill, covered, for 24 hours or longer.

Yield: 6 servings

SOUTHERN POTATO SALAD

This potato salad goes quickly at any gathering.

8 medium potatoes,
peeled, chopped
8 ounces medium
shrimp, cooked, peeled
1 rib celery, finely chopped
1 small onion, finely
chopped

2 tablespoons pimento
2 hard-cooked eggs, chopped
1/2 cup sour cream
1/2 cup mayonnaise
Salt and pepper to taste
Paprika

Combine the potatoes with enough water to cover in a saucepan. Bring to a boil. Boil until tender; drain. Combine the cooked potatoes, shrimp, celery, onion, pimento and eggs in a bowl and toss to mix. Combine the sour cream, mayonnaise, salt and pepper in a separate bowl and mix well. Add to the potato mixture and toss to coat. Spoon into a serving bowl. Sprinkle with paprika. Refrigerate , covered, until completely chilled.

Yield: 8 to 10 servings

BLACKEYED CHICKEN SALAD

Blackeyed peas add texture and flavor to this delightful salad.

1 (15-ounce) can blackeyed peas,
drained, rinsed, or 1 (10-ounce)
package frozen blackeyed peas,
cooked
1 1/2 cups chopped cooked
chicken
1 cup finely chopped carrot

1 cup finely chopped cucumber
1/4 cup finely chopped red onion
1/4 cup chopped fresh
mint leaves
1/2 cup Italian dressing
1 tablespoon Dijon mustard

Combine the peas, chicken, carrot, cucumber, red onion and mint in a bowl and mix well. Whisk the Italian dressing and mustard in a small bowl. Pour over the blackeyed pea mixture and toss to coat. Refrigerate, covered, for 4 to 5 hours. Spoon into a lettuce-lined bowl or onto a platter.

Yield: 6 servings

MONTEREY SALAD

2 cups shell pasta
2 cups chopped cooked ham
1/2 cup sliced green onions

2 cups seedless green grapes, sliced
Monterey Salad Dressing (below)

Cook the pasta using package directions. Rinse in cold water and drain. Combine the pasta, ham, green onions and green grapes in a bowl and mix well. Add the Monterey Salad Dressing and toss to coat. Refrigerate, covered, for 4 hours or longer.

Yield: 3 to 6 servings

CRAB AND WILD RICE SALAD

12 ounces broccoli
1/2 cup sliced carrot
1 (6-ounce) package long grain wild rice, cooked
8 medium fresh mushrooms
1/2 cup sliced zucchini
1/2 cup sliced yellow squash
1/2 cup sliced green onions

1/2 cup chopped red or green bell pepper
1/2 cup sliced black olives
2 hard-cooked eggs, finely chopped
1/2 cup plain yogurt
1/2 cup mayonnaise
1 pound lump crab meat

Cut the broccoli into florets. Bring a small amount of water to a boil in a saucepan. Add the broccoli and carrot. Cook for 5 minutes or until tender-crisp; drain. Mix with the rice, mushrooms, zucchini, squash, green onions, bell pepper, olives and eggs in a large bowl. Combine the yogurt and mayonnaise in a separate bowl and mix well. Pour over the rice mixture and toss to coat. Stir in the crab meat. Refrigerate, covered, for 4 to 6 hours. Garnish with lettuce leaves and tomato wedges.

Yield: 10 to 12 servings

MONTEREY SALAD DRESSING

Combine 1/2 cup mayonnaise, 1/2 cup sour cream, 2 tablespoons vinegar, 1 1/2 tablespoons Dijon mustard, 1 teaspoon sugar, pinch of cayenne, 1 tablespoon fresh dillweed and 1/4 teaspoon seasoned salt in a bowl and mix well.

FROM

HOPPIN' JOHN

TO

WILD RICE DRESSING

V E G E T A B L E S   A N D   S I D E   D I S H E S

THE VICTORIAN HOUSE

THE CITY MARKET

Any city needs to eat, and to meet this basic need, a regular market for Savannah was first established in Wright Square and, in 1763, moved to Ellis Square. Slaves were an important part of these markets, bringing fresh vegetables and other produce that they raised in their spare time into town from outlying plantations on Sundays. It was possible to buy any number of items at the market. Emily Burke, a schoolteacher writing in 1850, noted:

Here almost every eatable thing can be found. Vegetables fresh from the garden are sold the year round. All kinds of fish, both shell and finny, may be had there; birds of all kinds, both tame and wild, and the most delicious tropical fruits, as well as those which are brought from old countries. People travel a great distance for the purpose of buying and selling in this market.

A series of structures stood on Ellis Square, the last, built after the Civil War, housed room for 150 booths. The building could also be used for social events, such as the annual Southern Paper Ball. The building continued to show a profit into the 1950s, but after two years of wrangling over its future, the market was closed in 1953. A final costume ball was held to mark its passing. Seven hundred people attended, dressed as market mice, sacks of fertilizer, [in] nineteenth-century apparel, and the old market bell. The building was torn down and replaced with a parking garage.

The loss of the old market was a deep wound and served as a wake-up call for many Savannahians. The next time an historic structure was to be razed, again for a parking lot, a group of seven concerned women organized an effort to save it. They formed the Historic Savannah Foundation and saved the Davenport House, beginning a campaign to end the wanton destruction of Savannah's historic buildings.

"*People travel a great distance for the purpose of buying and selling in this market.*"

Feay Shellman Coleman, *Nostrums for Fashionable Entertainments: Dining in Georgia 1800–1850*. Savannah, Georgia: Telfair Academy of Arts and Sciences, Incorporated, 1992.

The Georgia Guardian. Savannah, Georgia, October 9, 1992.

BLACKEYED PEAS AND WINTER SQUASH

1 pound dried or $2^{1}/_{2}$ cups fresh
blackeyed peas
1 tablespoon vegetable oil
2 pounds winter squash, peeled,
seeded, chopped
2 large onions, chopped
Kernels of 4 ears fresh corn
2 large tomatoes, sliced
1 small chile, minced
3 to 6 garlic cloves, minced

1 tablespoon paprika
$1/_{2}$ teaspoon salt
1 teaspoon dried basil
1 tablespoon dried oregano
3 bay leaves
$1/_{4}$ teaspoon whole peppercorns
$1/_{2}$ teaspoon whole cumin seeds
$1/_{2}$ teaspoon whole
coriander seeds
$1/_{4}$ to $1/_{2}$ teaspoon chili powder

Rinse and sort the dried peas. Combine with enough water to cover in a bowl. Let stand for 8 hours or longer; drain. Place the peas in a large saucepan with enough water to cover. Bring to a simmer. Simmer for 20 minutes or until partially cooked. Remove from heat. Heat the oil in a large skillet. Add the squash, onions, corn, tomatoes, chile, garlic, paprika and salt. Cook for 10 minutes, stirring frequently. Add to the peas. Add enough water to cover. Add the basil, oregano, bay leaves, peppercorns, cumin, coriander and chili powder. Stir to combine. Bring to a simmer. Simmer, covered, for 25 minutes. Adjust the seasonings. Remove the bay leaves.

Yield: 16 servings

DOWN-HOME BLACKEYED PEAS AND COLLARD GREENS

3 cups blackeyed peas
1 ham hock
6 cups water
6 garlic cloves
$1^{1}/_{2}$ teaspoons salt

6 to 8 cups packed chopped
collard, mustard or turnip greens
2 medium leeks, chopped
Freshly ground pepper

Combine the peas, ham hock and water in a large pot. Bring to a boil. Reduce the heat. Simmer, covered, for 20 minutes, allowing the steam to escape and adding water $1/_{2}$ cup at a time if needed. Add the garlic. Simmer for an additional 15 minutes or until peas are tender. Add the salt, greens and leeks. Simmer until greens are tender. Remove ham hock. Season with pepper. Serve with corn bread.

Yield: 6 to 8 servings

ELVIRA'S FRIED BLACKEYED PEA PATTIES

1 (15-ounce) can blackeyed peas
1 large egg
$1/8$ teaspoon salt
$1/4$ teaspoon seasoned pepper

6 tablespoons (heaping) self-rising flour
$1^1/2$ cups chopped onion
$1/4$ cup vegetable oil

Mash the peas in a bowl. Add the egg, salt, pepper, flour and onion and mix well. Heat the oil in a skillet over medium-high heat. Drop the pea mixture by heaping tablespoonfuls into the hot oil. Cook until brown on both sides, turning once. Drain on paper towels.

Yield: 12 large patties

HOPPIN' JOHN

2 (10-ounce) packages frozen blackeyed peas
1 large onion, chopped
1 large green bell pepper, sliced
2 teaspoons garlic powder
1 teaspoon salt

1 tablespoon pepper
2 bay leaves
1 cup rice, cooked
8 ounces hot sausage, cooked, drained

Cook the peas with the onion, green pepper, garlic powder, salt, pepper and bay leaves in a saucepan using the package directions. Remove the bay leaves. Add the rice and sausage and mix well. Serve immediately.

Yield: 6 to 8 servings

"Ladies would go (to taverns) for dances but, as far as staying in them, that was a different story," Laing said. Taverns sold beer, wine and gin. But the most popular liquor, Weeks said, was rum—sold in a variety of drinks. Men often would buy rum punch—a blend of rum, water, spices and citrus—in large bowls and share them with the entire bar. Weeks said colonial Savannahians appear to be a people who gossiped freely, complained frequently about their government and enjoyed a good cocktail. "One of the things I've learned about Savannah and Savannahians from all this research," he said jokingly, "is that they haven't changed very much."

Excerpt from article of *Savannah News* 2/11/99

SHORELINE BEAN CASSEROLE

This will keep for several weeks. It is a different twist to baked beans.

1 pound summer sausage
8 ounces bacon, chopped
1 small onion, chopped
1 (16-ounce) can lima beans
1 (16-ounce) can butter beans

1 (16-ounce) can pork and beans
1 (16-ounce) can kidney beans
1/4 cup vinegar
1 cup packed brown sugar

Brown the sausage with the bacon and onion in an ovenproof skillet, stirring until the sausage is crumbly; drain. Drain the liquid from the cans of beans, reserving half. Stir the beans and reserved liquid into the sausage mixture. Combine the vinegar and brown sugar in a saucepan. Bring to a simmer. Simmer for 10 minutes. Add to the bean mixture and mix well. Bake at 350 degrees for 1 1/4 hours.

Yield: 16 to 20 servings

JONES STREET BROCCOLI FLORENTINE

1 large bunch broccoli, trimmed
2 (10-ounce) packages frozen chopped spinach, thawed
2 tablespoons butter
3 tablespoons flour
1 cup hot water

1 cup milk
2 egg yolks
1/2 cup white wine
Dash of nutmeg
1/4 cup grated Parmesan cheese
1/2 cup shredded Swiss cheese

Steam the broccoli in a steamer until tender-crisp; drain. Arrange in a 9x12-inch baking dish. Squeeze the spinach between paper towels to remove excess moisture. Arrange over the broccoli. Melt the butter in a saucepan. Stir in the flour. Add the hot water, milk, egg yolks, wine and nutmeg, whisking constantly. Cook over low heat until thickened. Pour over the spinach. Sprinkle with the Parmesan and Swiss cheeses. Bake at 450 degrees for 20 minutes.

Yield: 8 servings

CABBAGE ISLAND CASSEROLE

4 cups packed coarsely shredded
cabbage
1 cup celery, thinly sliced
1 cup boiling water
1/4 teaspoon salt
1 (10-ounce) can cream of celery
soup

4 teaspoons soy sauce
1/3 cup milk
1 tablespoon minced onion
Dash of Tabasco sauce
2 tablespoons butter
1/2 cup finely crushed butter
crackers

Combine the cabbage, celery, boiling water and salt in a saucepan. Boil, covered, for 5 minutes; drain. Combine the soup, soy sauce, milk, onion and Tabasco sauce in a 1 1/2-quart baking dish and mix well. Add the cabbage mixture and mix well. Melt the butter in a saucepan. Stir in the cracker crumbs. Sprinkle over the cabbage mixture. Bake at 350 degrees for 40 minutes or until bubbly and topping is browned.

Yield: 4 to 6 servings

LIVE OAK RED CABBAGE

2 tablespoons bacon drippings
4 cups shredded red cabbage
2 cups chopped apples
1/4 cup packed brown sugar

1/4 cup vinegar
1/4 cup water
1/4 teaspoon salt
1/2 teaspoon caraway seeds

Heat the bacon drippings in a skillet. Add the cabbage, apples, brown sugar, vinegar, water, salt and caraway seeds, stirring to combine. Cook for 25 to 30 minutes.

Yield: 4 to 6 servings

Indigenous substitutes were a hallmark of Confederate medicine. The forests and savannas were combed and every imaginable tonic, astringent, aromatic, and demulcent was prepared: cucumber for burns, pokeweed for camp itch, geranium for diarrhea, persimmons for dysentery and charcoal for diphtheria. The favorite, dubbed "old indigenous" contained dogwood bark, poplar bark, willow bark, and whiskey. And best of all, it was terrible bitter—just like quinine.
Excerpted from editorial found in the Special Collections Department of the
Medical College of Georgia Library.

ZESTY CARROT BAKE

Salt to taste
6 cups sliced carrots
1/2 cup finely chopped celery
1/4 cup finely chopped onion
2 tablespoons butter or margarine
2 tablespoons flour
1/4 teaspoon salt

1/4 teaspoon dry mustard
Dash of pepper
1 1/2 cups milk
1 cup shredded Cheddar cheese
2 tablespoons snipped parsley
1 1/2 cups soft bread crumbs
2 tablespoons butter or margarine, melted

Bring a small amount of salted water to a boil in a saucepan. Add the carrots. Cook for 12 minutes or until tender-crisp; drain. Set aside and keep warm. Cook the celery and onion in the butter in a skillet until tender. Stir in the flour, 1/4 teaspoon salt, mustard and pepper. Add the milk, whisking constantly. Cook over medium heat until thickened and bubbly, stirring constantly. Cook for 1 additional minute. Stir in the Cheddar cheese and parsley. Cook until cheese melts, stirring constantly. Arrange carrots in a 1 1/2-quart baking dish. Pour the cheese sauce over the carrots and stir to mix. Combine the bread crumbs and melted butter in a small bowl and mix well. Sprinkle over the carrot mixture. Bake at 350 degrees for 25 minutes or until heated through.

Yield: 8 servings

SURPRISE CORN PUDDING

2 (15-ounce) cans whole kernel corn, drained
1/4 cup flour
1 tablespoon cornmeal
3 tablespoons sugar
3 tablespoons butter or margarine, melted

3/4 cup milk
2 eggs
1/8 teaspoon cinnamon
1/8 teaspoon nutmeg
1/4 teaspoon vanilla extract (optional)

Process 1 can of corn in a blender until smooth, scraping down the sides. Combine with the remaining can of corn, flour, cornmeal, sugar and butter in a bowl and mix well. Whisk the milk, eggs, cinnamon, nutmeg and vanilla in a separate bowl. Stir into the corn mixture. Spoon into a greased shallow 2-quart baking dish. Bake at 350 degrees for 35 minutes or until set.

Yield: 8 servings

CORN AND RICE CASSEROLE

1 medium onion, chopped
1 green bell pepper, chopped
$1/2$ cup butter or margarine
1 (15-ounce) can whole kernel white corn
1 (15-ounce) can cream-style white corn

2 cups cooked rice
1 jalapeño pepper, chopped
1 teaspoon sugar
2 cups shredded sharp Cheddar cheese

Sauté the onion and green pepper in butter in a skillet until the onion is tender. Add the corn, rice, jalapeño pepper and sugar and mix well. Spoon into a 9x13-inch baking dish. Sprinkle with cheese. Bake at 350 degrees for 30 to 45 minutes.

Yield: 12 servings

SPICY COLLARD GREENS

In the South, people tend to be loyal to one green—turnip, mustard, or collard. It is important to watch when buying greens that there are not any yellow or discolored areas.

1 (2-pound) smoke-cured pork shoulder hock or 2 pounds sliced lean smoked country bacon, cut into 1-inch pieces
18 cups water
6 pounds collard greens
3 medium onions, coarsely chopped
6 tablespoons olive oil

$1^{1}/2$ tablespoons minced garlic
$1^{1}/2$ teaspoons crushed red pepper
$1/2$ teaspoon salt
$1/2$ teaspoon freshly ground black pepper
2 (28-ounce) cans whole peeled tomatoes, drained

Combine the pork shoulder hock and water in a stockpot. Bring to a boil. Cook, covered, for 2 hours over medium heat; strain. Refrigerate for 4 hours or longer. Skim off the fat. May be refrigerated for several days or frozen for 1 month. Remove the stems and ribs from the collard greens. Cut into 1-inch wide strips. Bring 8 cups of the stock to a boil in a large enameled cast-iron pot. Add the collard greens. Cook over medium-high heat for 30 to 40 minutes or until tender. Drain, reserving the liquid. Dry the pot. Add the onions and oil. Cook the onions for 5 to 6 minutes or until translucent. Add the garlic, red pepper, salt and black pepper. Cook for 1 minute, stirring constantly. Add the tomatoes and 3 cups of the reserved liquid. Simmer for 15 minutes or until tomatoes break up easily. Stir in the collard greens. Cook for 5 minutes or until heated through.

Yield: 12 servings

Msakwatas

Msakwatas means "broken into pieces." The dish is truly an indigenous one, given to the early settlers by the Indians. This recipe is adapted from the original.

1 (10-ounce) package frozen baby lima beans
1 (10-ounce) package frozen Shoe Peg white corn with butter sauce
2 tablespoons butter

$1/2$ teaspoon salt
$1/2$ teaspoon sugar
$1/4$ teaspoon pepper
1 cup half-and-half or whipping cream

Cook the lima beans in a saucepan using package directions; drain. Cook the corn using the package directions. Add to the lima beans and mix well. Add the butter, salt, sugar, pepper and half-and-half and mix well. Cook over low heat until of serving temperature.

Yield: 4 to 6 servings

Greek Onions

3 Vidalia onions
1 (10-ounce) package frozen chopped spinach, thawed
1 cup ricotta cheese
$1/2$ cup feta cheese
1 tablespoon Italian herbs

$1/4$ teaspoon cayenne
2 eggs, beaten
2 tablespoons flour
$1/2$ cup shredded Swiss or Parmesan cheese
4 slices bacon, cooked, crumbled

Cut the onions into $1/2$-inch thick slices. Arrange in the bottom of a 10-inch microwave-safe pie plate sprayed with nonstick cooking spray. Squeeze the spinach between paper towels to remove excess moisture. Combine the spinach, ricotta cheese, feta cheese, Italian herbs, cayenne, eggs and flour in a bowl and mix well. Spoon over the onions. Sprinkle with Swiss cheese and bacon. Microwave on High for 10 to 15 minutes, turning pie plate $1/4$ turn every 3 to 4 minutes. Let stand for 5 minutes. Cut into 6 slices.

Yield: 6 servings

SAVORY STUFFED VIDALIA ONIONS

4 large Vidalia onions, peeled
3 ounces cream cheese, softened
3 slices bacon, cooked, crumbled
1/4 cup chives
1/4 cup sliced mushrooms
1/2 teaspoon salt
1/4 teaspoon pepper

1/2 teaspoon garlic salt
2 drops of red pepper sauce
1/4 cup whipping cream
1/4 cup shredded Cheddar cheese
20 boiled shrimp
Chopped parsley to taste

Wrap each onion in a damp paper towel and place on a microwave-safe plate. Microwave on High for 10 minutes or until onions are tender. Spoon out the pulp, leaving 3 outer layers of onions; discard pulp. Place onion shells in a microwave-safe dish. Combine the cream cheese, bacon, chives, mushrooms, salt, pepper, garlic salt, red pepper sauce, whipping cream and Cheddar cheese in a bowl and mix well. Spoon equal amounts of the mixture into the onion shells. Microwave on High for 2 to 3 minutes or until heated through. Arrange 5 boiled shrimp around the top edge of each onion shell. Sprinkle with parsley.

Yield: 4 servings

VIDALIA ONION CUSTARD

3 cups sliced Vidalia onions
1/4 cup butter
1 cup shredded sharp cheese
3 eggs
1 cup milk
1/4 teaspoon pepper

1/2 teaspoon salt
1/4 teaspoon thyme
1/2 cup crushed cheese crackers
8 slices bacon, cooked, crumbled
Poppy seeds to taste

Sauté the onions in butter in a skillet until tender. Place in a greased 2-quart baking dish. Sprinkle the cheese over the onions. Beat the eggs and milk in a mixer bowl. Beat in the pepper, salt and thyme. Pour over the layers. Sprinkle with the cheese crackers, bacon and poppy seeds. Bake at 350 degrees for 30 minutes or until set.

Yield: 6 to 8 servings

BAKED PINEAPPLE CASSEROLE

This is so easy and great with roast beef or chicken.

5 slices bread
1 (20-ounce) can crushed pineapple
3 eggs, beaten

$^2/_3$ cup sugar
1 tablespoon flour
Pinch of salt
$^1/_2$ cup melted butter

Cube 3 slices of the bread and sprinkle over the bottom of a greased 2-quart baking dish. Combine the pineapple, eggs, sugar, flour and salt in a bowl and mix well. Spoon over the bread. Cube the remaining 2 slices bread and sprinkle over the pineapple mixture. Drizzle with the melted butter. Bake at 350 degrees for 45 minutes.

Yield: 9 servings

TONDEE'S POTATO CASSEROLE

This can be made 1 day ahead. It is rich and delicious.

2 cups mashed cooked potatoes
8 ounces cream cheese, softened
1 onion, chopped
2 eggs
2 tablespoons flour

Salt and pepper to taste
1 (6-ounce) can French-fried onions or 2 cups shredded Cheddar cheese

Beat the mashed potatoes, cream cheese, onion, eggs, flour, salt and pepper in a mixer bowl until light and fluffy. Spoon into a greased 8-inch square baking dish. May be refrigerated for 1 day. Bake at 300 degrees for 35 minutes. Sprinkle the French-fried onions over the top. Bake until the onions are browned.

Yield: 6 servings

SOUTHERN CREAMED POTATOES AND CARROTS

3 large potatoes, peeled, sliced
Salt and pepper to taste
2 tablespoons margarine

3 large carrots, peeled, sliced
1 teaspoon sugar
$1/2$ cup evaporated milk

Combine the potatoes with salt, pepper and enough water to cover in a saucepan. Bring to a boil. Boil until tender; drain. Cream the potatoes with 1 tablespoon of the margarine in a mixer bowl. Combine the carrots and sugar with enough water to cover in a saucepan. Bring to a boil. Boil until tender; drain. Cream the carrots with the remaining 1 tablespoon margarine in a mixer bowl. Add the creamed potatoes and evaporated milk to the carrot mixture. Beat for 5 minutes. *Variation:* May add 1 cup cooked chopped broccoli or spinach.

Yield: 6 to 8 servings

SQUASH BOATS FLORENTINE

8 yellow squash
1 (10-ounce) package frozen spinach
$1/4$ cup butter
$1/4$ cup light cream

1 teaspoon salt
$1/4$ teaspoon pepper
8 ounces crab meat
Buttered bread crumbs to taste
Grated Parmesan cheese to taste

Cut the stem ends from the squash. Steam in a steamer until almost tender; drain. Cut lengthwise and scoop out the pulp, reserving the shells and juices. Cook the spinach using the package directions; drain. Combine the cooked spinach, squash pulp, butter, cream, salt and pepper in a blender container. Process until smooth. Combine the squash mixture and crab meat in a bowl. Spoon into the squash shells. Sprinkle the bread crumbs and cheese over the top. Place squash shells on baking sheets. Bake at 350 degrees for 15 minutes. Place under a preheated broiler until brown.

Yield: 16 servings

BUTTERNUT SQUASH AND APPLES

1 butternut squash, chopped
4 apples, peeled, chopped
$^3/_4$ teaspoon cinnamon
$^1/_2$ cup packed brown sugar
2 tablespoons butter
$^1/_2$ cup apricot or orange juice

Layer the squash and apples alternately with the cinnamon, brown sugar and butter in a 9-inch square baking dish. Pour the juice over the layers. Bake at 350 degrees for 1 hour or until squash is tender.

Yield: 4 to 6 servings

CALICO SQUASH CASSEROLE

2 cups $^1/_4$-inch thick slices yellow squash
1 cup $^1/_4$-inch thick slices zucchini
1 medium onion, chopped
$^1/_4$ cup sliced green onions
1 cup water
1 teaspoon salt
2 cups crushed butter crackers
$^1/_2$ cup butter or margarine, melted
1 (10-ounce) can cream of chicken soup
1 (8-ounce) can sliced water chestnuts, drained
1 large carrot, shredded
$^1/_2$ cup mayonnaise
1 (2-ounce) jar diced pimento, drained
1 teaspoon rubbed sage or poultry seasoning
$^1/_2$ teaspoon white pepper (optional)
1 cup shredded sharp Cheddar cheese

Combine the yellow squash, zucchini, onion, green onions, water and $^1/_2$ teaspoon of the salt in a saucepan. Cook, covered, for 6 minutes or until squash is tender; drain. Combine the cracker crumbs and butter in a bowl and mix well. Spoon half the crumb mixture into a greased shallow $1^1/_2$-quart baking dish. Combine the soup, water chestnuts, carrot, mayonnaise, pimento, sage, white pepper and the remaining $^1/_2$ teaspoon salt in a bowl and mix well. Fold into the squash mixture. Spoon over the crumbs. Sprinkle the cheese and remaining crumb mixture over the top. Bake at 350 degrees for 30 minutes or until lightly browned.

Yield: 8 servings

Tybrisa Tomato Pudding

3 (10-ounce) cans tomato purée
1 1/2 cups packed brown sugar
1/2 teaspoon cloves
1/2 teaspoon pepper
1/4 teaspoon salt
1 (6-ounce) can spicy hot vegetable juice cocktail
12 slices white bread
3/4 cups butter, melted

Combine the tomato purée, brown sugar, cloves, pepper, salt and vegetable juice cocktail in a saucepan. Bring to a boil. Reduce the heat. Simmer for 5 minutes. Cut the bread into 1-inch cubes. Place the bread cubes in a buttered 9x12-inch baking dish. Pour the melted butter over the bread cubes. Pour the tomato mixture over the bread cubes. Bake, covered, at 375 degrees for 30 minutes. Bake, uncovered, for an additional 15 minutes.

Yield: 8 to 10 servings

The musical cry, "ye Georgia watermelons," and right on down the vegetable line to
"ye turnip greens," won for Lee Payne, 59-year old Negro huckster, and his mule Bill, "the
championship prize in the street criers contest held yesterday afternoon in the Park Extension.
The affair was sponsored by the Georgia Society of the Colonial Dames of America,
and was witnessed by a crowd of more than 1,000 persons who thronged both
sides of the walk between the band stand and the monument.
The winner of the grand prize was driving a dilapidated old milk truck pulled by the
aforementioned "Bill", whose protruding bones could easily have served as a hat rack."
Excerpt from *Savannah News* article titled Lee Payne's Mighty Blasts
Win Honors at Criers' Fair 4/7/34

Smithy's Turnip Green Casserole

2 cups turnip greens, cooked,
   drained, chopped, or
1 (16-ounce) package frozen
   turnip greens, thawed
1 (10-ounce) can cream of
   mushroom soup
1/2 cup mayonnaise
1 teaspoon horseradish

1 teaspoon sugar
3 tablespoons white wine vinegar
3 eggs, beaten
Salt and pepper to taste
1/4 cup bread crumbs, or to taste
1 cup shredded Cheddar cheese,
   or to taste

Preheat oven to 350 degrees. Combine the turnip greens, soup and mayonnaise in a bowl and mix well. Add the horseradish, sugar, vinegar and eggs and mix well. Season with salt and pepper. Spoon into a 9-inch square or 7x11-inch baking dish sprayed with nonstick cooking spray. Combine the bread crumbs and cheese in a bowl. Sprinkle over the top. Bake for 1 hour.

Yield: 10 servings

Yummy Yams

1 (16-ounce) can whole yams,
   drained
1/4 cup butter
1/2 cup bourbon
1/3 cup orange juice

1/4 cup packed brown sugar
Salt to taste
Cinnamon, nutmeg or allspice
   to taste

Place the yams in a buttered 8-inch square baking dish. Melt the butter in a saucepan. Add the bourbon, orange juice, brown sugar, salt and cinnamon and mix well. Pour over the yams. Bake at 350 degrees for 20 minutes or until bubbly.

Yield: 4 servings

RICE WITH WATER CHESTNUTS AND SAUSAGE

1 pound bulk hot sausage
1 cup rice
1 (8-ounce) can sliced water chestnuts

$^1/_4$ cup butter, softened
1 (4-ounce) can mushrooms
1 (10-ounce) can onion soup
5 ounces water

Brown the sausage in a skillet, stirring until crumbly; drain. Combine the cooked sausage, rice, water chestnuts, butter, mushrooms, soup and water in a bowl and mix well. Spoon into a 9-inch baking dish. Bake, covered, at 350 degrees for 30 minutes. Stir well. Bake, covered, for an additional 30 to 40 minutes or until rice is tender.

Yield: 6 to 8 servings

SAVANNAH RIVER RED RICE

1 cup tomato juice
$1^1/_2$ cups chicken broth
2 tablespoons tomato paste
$^1/_8$ teaspoon cayenne
$^1/_2$ teaspoon salt
$^1/_4$ teaspoon white pepper

$^1/_2$ cup chopped onion
$^1/_2$ cup finely chopped celery
$^1/_4$ cup chopped green bell pepper
6 tablespoons olive oil
2 cups parboiled rice

Combine the juice, broth, tomato paste, cayenne, salt and white pepper in a large ovenproof saucepan. Bring to a simmer. Sauté the onion, celery and green pepper in the oil in a skillet until tender. Stir in the rice, coating with oil. Add the rice mixture to the tomato mixture and mix well. Bring to a boil. Bake, covered, at 350 degrees or simmer for 20 to 25 minutes. *Variation:* May add 4 ounces hot cooked sausage before baking.

Yield: 6 servings

Wild Rice Dressing

1 cup wild rice
2 3/4 cups chicken broth
3/4 cup dry white wine or water
1/2 cup long grain rice
1 cup chopped shallots
1 cup chopped celery
2 tablespoons finely chopped gingerroot

2 tablespoons butter or margarine
3 cups seedless grapes, cut into halves
1/2 teaspoon salt
1/4 teaspoon pepper
3 tablespoons minced parsley
3 tablespoons almonds, toasted

Soak the wild rice in enough cold water to cover in a bowl for 2 hours, if you prefer rice that is less chewy; drain. Combine the broth and wine in a saucepan. Bring to a boil. Add the wild rice and long grain rice. Reduce the heat. Simmer, covered, for 35 to 45 minutes or until the liquid is absorbed. Sauté the shallots, celery and gingerroot in butter in a skillet until tender-crisp. Stir in the cooked rice, grapes, salt and pepper. Spoon rice mixture into a buttered 2 1/2-quart baking dish. Bake, covered, at 350 degrees for 25 to 30 minutes or until completely heated. Sprinkle with parsley and almonds.

Yield: 8 to 10 servings

Cheesy Palatial Puff

1/3 cup chopped onion
1 tablespoon butter
8 eggs
1 cup whole milk
2 teaspoons salt
1/4 teaspoon pepper

2 tablespoons chopped parsley
1 (10-ounce) package frozen green peas
8 ounces Swiss cheese, cut into thin strips

Cook the onion in butter in a skillet until tender. Combine the eggs, milk, salt and pepper in a bowl and mix well. Add the cooked onion and parsley to the egg mixture and mix well. Stir in the peas. Spoon into a buttered 1 1/2-quart baking dish. Top with the cheese. Bake at 350 degrees for 40 minutes.

Yield: 6 servings

FROM

BARBECUE PORK

TO

DUCK
STROGANOFF

MEATS AND POULTRY

THE
OLDE PINK HOUSE

THE AGELESS HALLS OF HABERSHAM

The Olde Pink House was formerly known as the Habersham House. The name was changed when the soft native brick began to bleed through the plastered walls and mysteriously changed the color from white to Jamaican pink. The stately Georgia Mansion was built on land granted by crown of England. James Habersham, Jr., lived in the mansion from 1771 to 1800 and held many secret meetings that helped secure the independence of the thirteen colonies from England.

In 1811, the Pink House became Planters Bank, the first bank in the State of Georgia. Used to house the monies of all the colonists in its massive cast-iron vaults with dungeon-like doors, the vaults are still in operation as wine cellars today.

In 1865, after Sherman's march to the sea and after he presented the city of Savannah as a Christmas gift to President Lincoln, General York set up headquarters in the Olde Pink Mansion.

The ageless Halls of Habersham (the Olde Pink House) echo the pleasure of dining by candlelight as was enjoyed by James Habersham, Jr., back in 1771. The ghosts of the past walk freely with you on your visit through the elegant rooms and wine vault cellars, up the fine staircases, or down for a drink by the massive Planters Tavern fires.

> *"In 1811, the Pink House became Planters Bank, the first bank in the State of Georgia."*

Provided by the staff of the Olde Pink House.

SPICY ORANGE POT ROAST

1 (5-pound) fresh beef brisket roast, chuck roast or London broil

1 tablespoon seasoned salt

1 teaspoon freshly ground pepper

2 tablespoons whole pickling spices, including red pepper pieces

3 large onions, thinly sliced

1 cup unsweetened orange juice

$^1/2$ cup sweet red wine

2 tablespoons catsup

1 tablespoon brown sugar

1 garlic clove, minced

Cornstarch

$^1/4$ cup cold water

Rub the brisket with seasoned salt, pepper and pickling spices. Place in a shallow dish. Refrigerate, covered, for 8 hours or longer. Arrange half the onion slices over the bottom of a 10x15-inch roasting pan. Place the brisket fat side up over the onions. Cover with remaining onions. Combine the orange juice, wine, catsup, brown sugar and garlic in a bowl and mix well. Pour over the roast. Bake at 325 degrees for 3 hours or until tender. Remove to a carving board; slice. Strain and skim the pan juices. Dissolve cornstarch in the cold water in a bowl, using 1 tablespoon of cornstarch for every $1^1/2$ to 2 cups of juices. Combine the pan juices and dissolved cornstarch in a saucepan. Cook over medium-high heat until of the desired consistency. Adjust the seasonings to taste. Serve the pot roast and gravy with rice.

Yield: 15 to 20 servings

BLAIR MEATBALL SAUCE

Combine $^1/4$ cup cranberry sauce, $^1/2$ cup chili sauce, 1 teaspoon (or more) lemon juice and 1 cup water in a saucepan and mix well. Bring to a boil. Boil for 1 minute. Pour over hot meatballs in a saucepan. Simmer until ready to serve.

FRENCH STEW

1 cup burgundy
1 envelope onion soup mix
1 (10-ounce) can cream of
mushroom soup
2 pounds beef stew meat
1/3 cup pimento-stuffed olives

1 (16-ounce) can tiny
whole carrots
1 (4-ounce) can tiny button
mushrooms
1 green bell pepper, chopped
1 (16-ounce) can small
whole onions

Combine the wine, soup mix and soup in a Dutch oven and mix well. Add the beef and stir to combine. Bake, covered, at 250 degrees for 4 hours, adding additional wine as needed. Stir in the olives, carrots, mushrooms, green pepper and onions. Bake, covered, for 1 hour longer, adding water or additional wine if needed. Chill for 1 day for enhanced flavor. Reheat before serving.

Yield: 6 to 8 servings

BLACKEYED PEAS AND GROUND BEEF STEW

8 ounces ground beef
1 small onion, chopped
2 tablespoons bacon drippings
2 cups cooked tomatoes

1 1/2 teaspoons salt
1 (10-ounce) package frozen
blackeyed peas

Brown the ground beef with the onion in the bacon drippings in a skillet, stirring until the ground beef is crumbly; drain. Stir in the tomatoes and salt. Stir in the blackeyed peas. Bring to a boil. Reduce the heat. Simmer for 30 minutes. Serve with French or Italian bread and a platter of fresh vegetables.

Yield: 4 to 6 servings

CREAM CHEESE LASAGNA

1 pound lean ground beef
1/2 cup chopped onion
1 (8-ounce) can tomato sauce
1 (6-ounce) can tomato paste
1 tablespoon parsley flakes
2 teaspoons Italian seasoning
1 teaspoon instant beef bouillon
1/4 teaspoon garlic powder
8 ounces cream cheese, softened

1 cup ricotta cheese
1/4 cup sour cream
2 eggs, beaten
8 ounces lasagna noodles, cooked
1 (4-ounce) package sliced pepperoni
1/2 cup grated Parmesan cheese
2 cups shredded mozzarella cheese

Brown the ground beef with the onion in a skillet, stirring until the ground beef is crumbly; drain. Stir in the tomato sauce, tomato paste, parsley flakes, Italian seasoning, instant bouillon and garlic powder. Bring to a boil. Reduce the heat. Simmer for 1 hour. Combine the cream cheese, ricotta cheese, sour cream and eggs in a bowl and mix well. Layer half the meat sauce, half the noodles, the cream cheese mixture, pepperoni, Parmesan cheese, mozzarella cheese, remaining noodles and remaining meat sauce over the bottom of a greased 8x12-inch baking dish. Bake, covered, at 350 degrees for 30 minutes.

Yield: 10 servings

The passengers ate beef aboard Oglethorpe's ship "Anne" for four days a week, pork two days and fish one day. Everyone, children included, drank beer, although it was probably more like cider than today's brew. Some vegetables—carrots, potatoes and onions—were given out along with bread, butter and molasses. Ill passengers were given sage tea, water gruel with sugar, white wine and fresh broth that Oglethorpe had made from his own supplies.

Excerpt from article of *Savannah News* 1/21/99

COBBLESTONE BEEF CASSEROLE

*This recipe was adapted from one in another cookbook. It did not
contain corn bread twists, but this feature gives it a decidedly Mexican flavor.
It is hearty "comfort food."*

1¹/2 pounds ground beef
1 teaspoon salt
1 (16-ounce) can pork and beans
³/4 cup barbecue sauce

2 tablespoons brown sugar
1 tablespoon dried minced onion
1 (8-count) can corn bread twists
1 cup shredded Cheddar cheese

Brown the ground beef in a skillet, stirring until crumbly; drain. Add the salt, pork and beans, barbecue sauce, brown sugar and onion and mix well. Cook over medium heat until mixture is heated through. Pour into a 9x13-inch baking dish. Arrange the corn bread twists diagonally over the ground beef mixture in a pattern. Sprinkle the Cheddar cheese over the top. Bake at 375 degrees for 25 to 30 minutes or until the corn bread is browned and the cheese is melted.

Yield: 8 servings

MEXICAN MEAT LOAF

1 pound lean ground beef
1 cup rolled oats
1 cup chunky picante sauce
or salsa

1 egg
Pinch of salt
Pinch of pepper

Combine the ground beef, oats, picante sauce, egg, salt and pepper in a bowl and mix well. Press into a greased 5x9-inch loaf pan. Bake at 350 degrees for 1 hour or until cooked through.

Yield: 4 to 6 servings

Sweet-and-Sour Meat Loaf

This recipe is from the extensive collection of an excellent cook.

1 (15-ounce) can tomato sauce
1 teaspoon mustard
$^1/_4$ cup vinegar
$^1/_2$ cup packed brown sugar
8 ounces ground pork
2 pounds lean ground beef
$^1/_2$ cup fine soft bread crumbs
2 eggs, lightly beaten
$^1/_2$ cup minced onion
1 tablespoon salt
$^1/_4$ teaspoon pepper

Combine the tomato sauce, mustard, vinegar and brown sugar in a bowl and mix well. Combine the ground pork, ground beef, bread crumbs, eggs, onion, salt and pepper in a separate bowl and mix well. Add 1 cup of the tomato sauce mixture and mix well. Press into a $1^1/_2$-quart baking dish or loaf pan. Pour $^1/_4$ cup of the tomato sauce mixture over the top. Bake at 350 degrees for $1^1/_2$ hours or until cooked through. Heat the remaining tomato sauce mixture and serve with the meat loaf.
Variations: Add olives, cheese or mushrooms to the ground beef mixture or press half of the ground beef mixture into the baking dish, place a row of hard-cooked eggs or a "log" of cheese in the center and cover with the remaining ground beef mixture.

Yield: 8 to 10 servings

Colonist Elisha Dobee wrote numerous pleading letters to the Trustees. In January 1735 he wrote: "As we have no fresh beef nor pork out of the Store, eating so much salt meat heats the blood and causes the scurvy . . . "
Page 20, Excerpt from Edward Chang Sieg, *Eden on the Marsh: An Illustrated History of Savannah, 1985.* Windsor Publications.

ST. PATTY'S REUBEN CASSEROLE

2 cups cream of chicken soup
1/4 cup mayonnaise
4 teaspoons mustard
4 cups sauerkraut, drained
8 ounces noodles, cooked

12 ounces corned beef
1/2 cup chopped onion
3/4 cup shredded Swiss cheese
1/2 cup rye bread crumbs

Combine the soup, mayonnaise and mustard in a bowl and mix well. Layer the sauerkraut, noodles, soup mixture, corned beef, onion, cheese and bread crumbs in a baking dish. Bake at 350 degrees for 45 minutes or until cooked through.

Yield: 6 to 8 servings

LEG OF LAMB

1/2 cup water
1/3 cup vinegar
3 tablespoons Worcestershire sauce
2 teaspoons Dijon mustard

1 teaspoon garlic salt
Dash of cayenne
1 (5-pound) leg of lamb
3/4 cup bread crumbs

Combine the water, vinegar, Worcestershire sauce, mustard, garlic salt and cayenne in a bowl and mix well. Place the lamb in a roasting pan. Spoon the sauce over the lamb, reserving a small amount. Roast at 350 degrees for 2 hours, basting every 30 minutes with the remaining sauce. Sprinkle the lamb with the bread crumbs. Roast for 30 minutes longer or until lamb registers 175 to 180 degrees on a meat thermometer, covering if needed.

Yield: 6 servings

Lamb Shanks and Rice

This dish is typical of French cookery, because of bones and the flavor they add.

1 garlic head	2 green bell peppers, chopped
4 lamb shanks, cut into halves	2 cups water
Flour to taste	1 cup red wine
Salt and pepper to taste	4 bay leaves
Vegetable oil	1 tablespoon salt
1 cup chopped onion	2 cups rice

Cut 4 cloves of garlic into slivers. Cut slits into the lamb shanks with a small knife. Insert the garlic slivers. Combine flour, salt and pepper to taste in a shallow dish and mix well. Dredge the lamb in the flour mixture, coating both sides. Brown the lamb in a small amount of oil in a skillet. Combine the lamb, onion, green peppers, the remaining garlic cloves, 1 cup of the water, wine, bay leaves and 1 tablespoon salt in a 2-quart baking dish. Bake, covered, at 350 degrees for $1^1/2$ hours or until the lamb begins to separate from the bone. Add the rice and remaining 1 cup water. Bake for an additional 30 to 45 minutes or until the rice is tender. Remove the bay leaves.

Yield: 4 to 6 servings

Barbecue Sauce

Combine $1/4$ cup lemon juice, $1/4$ cup water, $1/4$ cup sherry, $1/4$ cup chopped onion, $1/4$ cup raisins, $1/8$ teaspoon allspice and $1/8$ teaspoon cayenne in a saucepan and mix well. Bring to a boil. Simmer for 20 minutes. Stir in $1/4$ cup water, $1/4$ cup packed brown sugar and $1/2$ cup prepared barbecue sauce. Simmer for 10 minutes.

MEDALLIONS OF VENISON WITH MADEIRA SAUCE

8 venison tenderloins, trimmed
16 to 24 bacon slices

Madeira Sauce

Cover the tenderloins with the bacon slices. Place on a grill over hot coals. Cook until medium-rare; do not overcook. Remove to a serving platter. Cut into thin slices. Cover with Madeira Sauce. Garnish with seedless red grapes.

Yield: 8 servings

MADEIRA SAUCE

5 tablespoons butter
2 tablespoons flour
1 beef bouillon cube
1 cup boiling water
2 tablespoons port

8 ounces portobello mushrooms, sliced
3 shallots, chopped
$1/3$ cup madeira
Dash of Cognac

Melt 2 tablespoons of the butter in a saucepan. Combine the flour and a small amount of water in a bowl and mix until smooth. Pour into the melted butter, stirring to blend. Dissolve the bouillon cube in the boiling water. Add to the butter mixture. Bring to a boil, stirring constantly. Reduce the heat. Stir in the port. Simmer. Sauté the mushrooms and shallots in the remaining 3 tablespoons butter in a skillet until tender. Remove the cooked mushrooms and shallots with a slotted spoon and stir into the sauce. Add the madeira and Cognac. Simmer until of the desired consistency.

SLOW-COOKER BARBECUE PORK

*This recipe is good during the winter and just about cooks itself. Great for working
moms and dads without a lot of time on their hands.*

1 (3-pound) Boston butt pork roast	Coarsely chopped onion (optional)
6 whole cloves	1/2 to 1 cup barbecue sauce
1 cup water	Hamburger buns
2 onions, sliced	

Place the pork roast, cloves, water and sliced onions in a slow cooker. Cook on Low for 8 to 12 hours. Remove the roast. Reserve 1/2 cup of the liquid, discarding the remaining liquid, cloves and sliced onions. Remove the bone and fat from the roast. Shred the meat. Place the shredded meat, chopped onion, reserved liquid and barbecue sauce in the slow cooker. Cook on Low for 6 to 8 hours. Spoon into hamburger buns.

Yield: 6 servings

JOHNNY'S PORK ROAST

6 large mushrooms, sliced	1 tablespoon soy sauce
1 garlic clove, minced	1 (10-ounce) can French onion soup in beef broth
3 tablespoons margarine	
1 (2-pound) extra-lean pork roast	1 teaspoon lemon juice

Sauté the mushrooms and garlic in margarine in a skillet until tender. Cut a slit in the pork roast. Stuff with the mushroom mixture. Place slit side down in a roasting pan. Combine the soy sauce, soup and lemon juice in a bowl and mix well. Pour over the pork roast. Bake at 375 degrees for 1 hour and 20 minutes or until cooked through.

Yield: 6 servings

Baked Pork Chops with Cranberry Sauce

2 chicken bouillon cubes
3/4 cup boiling water
3 tablespoons brown sugar
3 tablespoons vinegar
1 (8-ounce) can sliced syrup-pack pineapple
3/4 cup whole cranberry sauce
6 (3/4-inch thick) pork chops
Salt and pepper to taste
1 tablespoon shortening
1 green bell pepper, cut into rings
3 tablespoons cornstarch
3 tablespoons water

Dissolve the bouillon in the boiling water in a small bowl. Stir in the brown sugar and vinegar. Drain the pineapple reserving the syrup. Combine the reserved syrup with the cranberry sauce in a bowl and mix well. Add the cranberry mixture to the bouillon mixture and mix well. Season the pork chops with salt and pepper. Melt the shortening in a skillet. Brown the pork chops in the hot shortening. Pour the cranberry mixture over the pork chops. Simmer, covered, for 50 minutes or until cooked through. Top each pork chop with a pineapple slice and a green pepper ring. Cook, covered, for an additional 10 minutes. Remove the pork chops to a warm serving platter. Combine the cornstarch and water in a cup and stir until smooth. Add to the sauce. Cook until mixture is of the desired consistency, stirring constantly. Pour over the pork chops.

Yield: 6 servings

Simply Delicious Pork Chops

2 tablespoons catsup
2 tablespoons vegetable oil
1 tablespoon Worcestershire sauce
1 tablespoon soy sauce
1 tablespoon lemon juice
4 pork chops

Combine the catsup, vegetable oil, Worcestershire sauce, soy sauce and lemon juice in a bowl and mix well. Place the pork chops in a 9x13-inch baking pan. Pour half the sauce over the pork chops. Bake at 350 degrees for 30 minutes. Turn the pork chops. Pour the remaining sauce over the top. Bake for an additional 30 minutes or until cooked through.

Yield: 4 servings

PORK CHOPS SAVANNAH STYLE

6 thick-cut pork chops	3 tablespoons flour
1/4 teaspoon salt	2 cups hot water
1/4 teaspoon sage	1 tablespoon vinegar
3 apples, thinly sliced	1/2 teaspoon salt
1/4 cup packed brown sugar	1/2 cup raisins

Sprinkle the pork chops with salt and sage. Brown on both sides in a skillet over medium-low heat. Remove the pork chops and place in a single layer in a baking dish. Arrange the apples over the top. Sprinkle with brown sugar. Stir the flour into the pork chop drippings. Add the hot water, whisking constantly. Stir until mixture thickens. Stir in the vinegar, salt and raisins. Pour over the pork chops. Bake, covered, at 350 degrees for 30 minutes or until cooked through.

Yield: 6 servings

BAKED HAM DIJON

1 (6-ounce) jar Dijon mustard	1 (8-ounce) jar honey
1 (12-ounce) can cola	1 (5- to 10-pound) bone-in ham

Combine the mustard, cola and honey in a bowl and whisk until thick and creamy. Trim the ham if desired. Place the ham in a large brown paper cooking bag. Place in a roasting pan. Pour the mustard mixture over the ham. Tie the bag closed and cut slits in the top. Bake at 350 degrees for 3 to 4 hours or until cooked through.

Yield: Variable

Ham and Cheese Pie

2 tablespoons butter
2 tablespoons flour
$1/2$ teaspoon salt
$1/8$ teaspoon nutmeg
$1^1/2$ cups milk

1 cup shredded Swiss cheese
3 eggs, slightly beaten
1 cup chopped cooked ham
1 deep-dish pie pastry shell

Melt the butter over low heat in a saucepan. Stir in the flour, salt and nutmeg. Add the milk, whisking constantly. Cook until the sauce has thickened, stirring constantly. Stir in the Swiss cheese gradually, cooking until melted. Stir a small amount of the sauce into the beaten eggs in a bowl; stir the eggs into the sauce. Add the ham and mix well. Bake the pastry shell at 425 degrees for 15 minutes. Reduce the heat to 300 degrees. Pour the ham mixture into the hot baked pie crust. Bake for 40 minutes or until set.

Yield: 5 to 6 servings

Factor's Walk Bacon Pie

12 slices bacon, cooked,
crumbled
1 cup shredded Cheddar cheese
$1/3$ cup chopped onion

2 cups milk
1 cup baking mix
$1/4$ teaspoon salt
$1/8$ teaspoon pepper

Sprinkle the bacon, cheese and onion over the bottom of a greased 9-inch pie plate. Combine the milk, baking mix, salt and pepper in a blender container. Process at high speed for 1 minute. Spoon over the onion mixture. Bake at 400 degrees for 35 to 40 minutes or until set. Let stand for 5 minutes.

Yield: 6 servings

COMPANY'S COMIN' BOURBON AND PEACH-GLAZED CHICKEN

1 (3^1/4- to 4-pound) chicken   Bourbon and Peach Glaze

Place the chicken breast side up on a rack in a roasting pan. Set aside ^{1}/4 cup of the Bourbon and Peach Glaze. Spoon the remaining glaze over the chicken. Bake at 375 degrees for 45 to 60 minutes or until chicken is golden brown, basting occasionally and adding water as needed to prevent juices from burning. Cover chicken loosely with foil. Bake an additional 30 to 45 minutes or until cooked through, basting occasionally. Remove chicken to a serving platter. Skim and discard the fat from the pan drippings. Combine the pan drippings with the reserved Bourbon and Peach Glaze in a saucepan. Bring to a boil over medium-high heat. Serve with the chicken.

Yield: 4 to 6 servings

BOURBON AND PEACH GLAZE

^{1}/2 cup peach preserves   1 teaspoon Worcestershire sauce
2 tablespoons butter ^{1}/2 teaspoon dry mustard
2 tablespoons bourbon or ^{1}/2 teaspoon salt
    orange juice ^{1}/8 teaspoon pepper

Combine the preserves, butter, bourbon, Worcestershire sauce, mustard, salt and pepper in a saucepan; mix well. Cook over medium heat until the butter is melted, stirring constantly.

HONEY BARBECUE SAUCE

Combine ^{1}/2 cup honey, 2 tablespoons soy sauce, 1 teaspoon mustard, 1 garlic clove, 1 cup chicken broth, ^{1}/4 cup catsup, ^{1}/2 teaspoon salt and ^{1}/4 teaspoon pepper in a blender container. Process until smooth. Pour over chicken or pork in a shallow dish. Marinate at room temperature for 1 hour.

"Track" Chicken

This is an excellent baked chicken recipe. Most of the fat cooks away, leaving the chicken tender and juicy with a crispy crust. Incredibly easy!

1 (2- to 2½-pound) chicken   ¼ cup salt

Rinse the chicken and pat dry. Make a 2-inch wide track of salt diagonally across an 8x8-inch baking pan. Place the chicken breast side down over the salt. Bake for 1 hour or until the chicken is cooked through and the skin is brown and crisp.

Yield: 2 to 4 servings

Chippewa Chicken and Sausage Casserole

¼ cup vegetable oil
1 medium chicken, cut up
1½ pounds Italian sausage
2 medium onions, sliced
4 green bell peppers, sliced
6 carrots, chopped

4 large potatoes, cut into quarters
Salt and pepper to taste
Garlic powder to taste
Oregano to taste

Spread a small amount of the oil over the bottom of a 9x13-inch baking pan. Layer the chicken pieces, sausage, onions, green peppers, carrots and potatoes in the prepared pan. Sprinkle the salt, pepper, garlic powder and oregano over the layers. Drizzle with the remaining oil. Bake, covered, at 375 degrees for 1 hour or until chicken is cooked through. Bake, uncovered, until browned.

Yield: Variable

EASY SWEET-AND-SOUR CHICKEN

1 medium package chicken parts
1 (8-ounce) bottle French salad dressing
1 (12-ounce) jar pineapple preserves
1 envelope onion soup mix

Arrange the chicken parts in a single layer in a buttered baking dish. Combine the salad dressing, preserves and soup mix in a bowl and mix well. Spoon over the chicken parts. Bake at 350 degrees for 1 hour or until cooked through.

Yield: Variable

LOUIE'S CHICKEN SPAGHETTI

This is from a Greek immigrant who made this delicious dish every week. It was a big favorite.

1 medium chicken, cut up
Flour
3 tablespoons olive oil
1 large onion, chopped
1 green bell pepper, chopped
1 tablespoon minced garlic
Garlic salt to taste
Pepper to taste
Oregano to taste
2 (14-ounce) cans stewed tomatoes, chopped
2 (17-ounce) jars spaghetti sauce
1 (6-ounce) can tomato paste
1 cup water
Hot cooked spaghetti noodles
Grated Parmesan cheese to taste

Coat the chicken lightly with flour. Brown the chicken in hot olive oil in a skillet on all sides. Remove the chicken and place in a Dutch oven. Drain the oil from the skillet, reserving 1 tablespoon. Sauté the onion, green pepper and garlic in the reserved oil in the skillet until tender. Spoon over the chicken. Sprinkle with garlic salt, pepper and oregano. Add the stewed tomatoes, spaghetti sauce, tomato paste and water and mix well. Simmer, covered, for 30 minutes, stirring frequently. Serve over the noodles. Sprinkle with Parmesan cheese.

Yield: 6 to 8 servings

BAY STREET CHICKEN ROLLS

Boneless chicken breasts are wrapped around an exotic blend of wild rice and pecans and flavored with a touch of sherry.

1 (6-ounce) package long grain wild rice mix
$^1/_4$ cup chopped pecans
$^1/_4$ cup sherry or apple juice
1 (4-ounce) can mushroom stems and pieces, drained
$^1/_4$ cup butter
$^1/_3$ cup finely crushed cornflakes
2 tablespoons dried parsley flakes
$^1/_2$ teaspoon salt
$^1/_2$ teaspoon rubbed sage
$^1/_2$ teaspoon dried thyme leaves
8 (4-ounce) boneless skinless chicken breasts

Prepare the rice using the package directions. Combine the prepared rice, pecans, sherry and mushrooms in a bowl and mix well. Preheat the oven to 350 degrees. Place the butter in a 3-quart baking dish. Heat in the oven for 5 to 7 minutes or until the butter is melted. Combine the cornflakes, parsley, salt, sage and thyme in a shallow dish and mix well. Pound the chicken breasts to $^1/_4$-inch thickness between sheets of waxed paper. Place 2 tablespoons of the rice mixture on each chicken breast. Roll up the chicken breasts, securing with wooden picks. Dip each roll into the melted butter. Roll in the cornflake mixture. Place seam side down in the buttered baking dish. Spoon remaining rice mixture around the chicken. Sprinkle remaining cornflake mixture over the chicken and rice. Bake for 35 to 45 minutes or until chicken is cooked through. *Tip:* Chicken rolls can be prepared ahead and refrigerated, covered, for up to 6 hours.

Yield: 8 servings

Do you remember when . . . "The Chatham Artillery had a Fourth of July picnic at Rose Dhu and every member and guest aimed the cannon, fired at a target across the marsh, and every one hit the bull's-eye, and all would celebrate each shot?"

BLACK TIE BROCCOLI AND CHICKEN

2 tablespoons margarine
or butter

4 boneless skinless chicken
breasts, cut into thin strips

2 cups broccoli florets

1 small red bell pepper, cut into
thin strips

1 cup chicken broth

1/2 teaspoon garlic powder

1/4 teaspoon pepper

3 ounces cream cheese,
softened

6 ounces bow tie pasta,
cooked, hot

Melt the margarine in a large skillet over medium heat. Add the chicken. Cook for 3 minutes or until chicken is white, stirring frequently. Remove the chicken to a warm plate and cover. Add the broccoli, red pepper, broth, garlic powder and pepper to the skillet. Cook, covered, for 5 to 7 minutes or until broccoli is tender-crisp, stirring occasionally. Stir in the chicken. Cook for 1 minute. Remove from heat. Add the cream cheese. Stir until cream cheese is melted. Add the pasta and toss to coat.

Yield: 4 servings

BOURBON CHICKEN

4 chicken breasts

1/2 cup soy sauce

1/2 cup packed brown sugar

1/2 teaspoon garlic powder

1 teaspoon ginger

2 tablespoons dried onion flakes

6 tablespoons bourbon, or
to taste

Arrange the chicken in a single layer in a shallow pan. Combine the soy sauce, brown sugar, garlic powder, ginger, onion flakes and bourbon in a bowl and mix well. Pour over the chicken. Marinate, covered, in the refrigerator for 8 hours or longer. Drain the chicken reserving the marinade. Place the chicken in a baking pan. Bake at 325 degrees for 1 1/2 hours or until browned and cooked through, basting frequently with the reserved marinade. Serve with rice.

Yield: 4 servings

BRIE-STUFFED CHICKEN BREASTS

1 medium onion, chopped
2 tablespoons olive oil
1 Granny Smith apple, coarsely chopped
1 teaspoon thyme
1 teaspoon salt
$1/2$ teaspoon pepper
$3/4$ cup apple cider
4 ounces Brie cheese, rind removed, chopped
4 chicken breast halves

Cook the onion in the olive oil in a skillet for 8 minutes or until tender. Add the apple, $1/2$ teaspoon of the thyme, $1/4$ teaspoon of the salt, $1/4$ teaspoon of the pepper and $1/4$ cup of the cider. Cook for 5 minutes or until apples are tender. Remove from heat and cool slightly. Stir in the Brie cheese. Separate the skin from the meat on each chicken breast. Place $1/4$ of the stuffing between the skin and the meat on each chicken breast, pressing gently to distribute the stuffing evenly. Season the chicken with $1/2$ teaspoon salt and remaining $1/4$ teaspoon pepper. Place in a 9x13-inch baking dish. Bake at 400 degrees for 35 minutes or until cooked through. Remove the chicken to a platter and keep warm. Skim the pan drippings. Scrape the drippings into a small saucepan. Add the remaining $1/2$ cup cider. Cook over medium heat until mixture is reduced by half. Stir in the remaining $1/2$ teaspoon thyme and $1/4$ teaspoon salt. Spoon over the chicken.

Yield: 4 servings

MUSTARD SAUCE

Combine $3/4$ cup mayonnaise, $1/4$ cup sour cream, 2 tablespoons prepared mustard, 1 tablespoon dry mustard, $1/3$ cup packed brown sugar and $1/4$ teaspoon salt in a jar. May add 1 drop of Tabasco sauce and $1/2$ to 1 teaspoon horseradish if desired. Shake to mix. Store in the refrigerator. This will keep for several weeks.

CACCIATORE

4 boneless skinless chicken breast halves
1 medium onion, sliced
1 medium green bell pepper, cut into strips
1 cup sliced mushrooms

2 tablespoons vegetable oil
1 envelope Italian, Mild Italian or Zesty Italian salad dressing mix
1 (28-ounce) can crushed tomatoes

Brown the chicken on both sides with the onion, green pepper and mushrooms in hot oil in a skillet, stirring frequently. Sprinkle the salad dressing mix over the chicken. Stir in the tomatoes. Bring to a boil. Reduce the heat to low. Simmer, covered, for 15 minutes, stirring occasionally. Serve over hot cooked pasta.

Yield: 4 servings

CHATHAM BAKED CHICKEN BREASTS

4 boneless chicken breast halves or 1 chicken, cut up
1/4 cup butter, melted
1/2 cup honey

1/2 teaspoon salt
1/4 cup Dijon mustard
1 teaspoon curry powder

Arrange the chicken in a baking dish. Combine the butter, honey, salt, mustard and curry powder in a bowl and mix well. Pour over the chicken. Bake at 325 degrees for 45 to 50 minutes or until chicken is golden brown and cooked through. Serve with rice or mashed potatoes.

Yield: 4 servings

CHICKEN BREASTS STUFFED WITH CRAB DRESSING

6 chicken breasts
Butter to taste
Salt and pepper to taste
1/4 cup catsup
1/4 cup butter, melted

2 tablespoons sherry
Dash of garlic powder
Dash of oregano
Crab Dressing

Spread a small amount of butter over each chicken breast. Sprinkle with salt and pepper. Place in a baking pan. Bake at 350 degrees for 30 minutes. Combine the catsup, melted butter, sherry, garlic powder and oregano in a bowl and mix well. Pour over the chicken breasts. Bake for an additional 10 minutes. Stuff the cavity of each chicken breast with 1/6 of the Crab Dressing. Bake for an additional 15 minutes or until browned and cooked through.

Yield: 6 servings

CRAB DRESSING

5 slices bread, torn into pieces
1 egg
Salt and pepper to taste
1/2 cup crab meat

Dash of sage
1 teaspoon minced onion
Chicken broth

Combine the bread, egg, salt, pepper, crab meat, sage and onion in a bowl and mix well. Add enough broth to moisten well.

Dinner traditionally was at 2:00 PM, followed occasionally by Madeira "tastings."
Betsy Fancher—Book, *Savannah: A Renaissance of the Heart*

Chicken Roll-Ups with Georgia Peanut Sauce

2 cups coleslaw mix
$^1/_2$ cup thinly sliced
green onions
3 tablespoons soy sauce
1$^1/_2$ teaspoons finely
chopped garlic
1 teaspoon finely chopped
gingerroot

$^1/_4$ teaspoon coarsely
ground pepper
4 (4-ounce) boneless skinless
chicken breasts
1 tablespoon butter
$^1/_4$ cup water
Peanut Sauce
Cilantro leaves

Combine the coleslaw mix, green onions, 2 tablespoons of the soy sauce, garlic, gingerroot and pepper in a bowl and mix well. Pound the chicken breasts to $^1/_4$-inch thickness between sheets of waxed paper. Place $^1/_4$ of the coleslaw mixture on each chicken breast. Roll up the chicken, securing with wooden picks. Melt the butter in a skillet until sizzling. Add the chicken. Cook over medium-high heat for 7 to 9 minutes or until golden brown on all sides. Combine the remaining 1 tablespoon soy sauce and water in a bowl and mix well. Pour over the chicken roll-ups. Reduce the heat. Cook, covered, until chicken is cooked through. Place roll-ups on a serving platter. Pour the Peanut Sauce over the top. Sprinkle with cilantro leaves.

Yield: 4 servings

PEANUT SAUCE

$^1/_4$ cup chopped unsalted
dry-roasted peanuts
$^1/_4$ cup sugar
$^1/_4$ cup soy sauce

2 tablespoons white vinegar
$^1/_4$ to $^1/_2$ teaspoon crushed
red pepper
1 to 3 teaspoons water (optional)

Combine the peanuts, sugar, soy sauce, vinegar and red pepper in a bowl and mix well. Stir in enough water to make of the desired consistency.

Evenings are apt to be long and carefree for Savannahians love a party and are
loath to leave one. This is a city that prizes good food and good drink
as basic to the good life, and it takes its pleasures seriously.

Betsy Fancher—Book, *Savannah: A Renaissance of the Heart*

Chicken Dijon

4 chicken breasts

2 tablespoons butter

$^1/_2$ teaspoon salt

1 small bay leaf

$^1/_2$ cup sauterne or white wine of choice

Pinch of cayenne

$^1/_4$ teaspoon tarragon

$^1/_4$ teaspoon thyme

2 egg yolks, beaten

2 tablespoons sour cream

2 tablespoons Dijon mustard

Brown the chicken on both sides in the butter in a skillet. Add the salt, bay leaf, wine, cayenne, tarragon and thyme. Bring to a boil. Reduce the heat. Simmer for 45 minutes. Discard the bay leaf. Remove the chicken to a warm serving platter. Reduce the heat to low. Stir a small amount of the hot liquid into the beaten egg yolks. Add the egg yolks to the hot liquid, whisking constantly. Add the sour cream and mustard. Cook until thickened, stirring constantly. Pour over the chicken. Serve with hot fluffy rice or noodles.

Yield: 4 servings

Chicken Tortilla Casserole

3 chicken breasts, boned

1 (4-ounce) can chopped green chiles

1 (10-ounce) can cream of chicken soup

1 (10-ounce) can cream of mushroom soup

1 egg

Salt and pepper to taste

1 onion, chopped (optional)

2 cups shredded mild Cheddar cheese

2 cups shredded Monterey Jack cheese

6 corn tortillas, cut into quarters

Combine the chicken with enough water to cover in a saucepan. Bring to a boil. Reduce the heat. Simmer until cooked through; drain. Chop the cooked chicken. Combine the chiles, chicken soup, mushroom soup, egg, salt, pepper and onion in a bowl and mix well. Place the Cheddar cheese and Monterey Jack cheese in a bowl and toss to combine. Layer the tortillas, soup mixture, chicken and cheeses alternately in a 2-quart baking dish until all ingredients are used, ending with the cheeses. Bake at 350 degrees for 1 hour. *Variation:* Add 1 can cream of broccoli soup to the soup mixture and add a layer of broccoli florets.

Yield: 6 servings

THIRTY-MINUTE CHUTNEY CHICKEN

4 ounces orzo or noodles

2 tablespoons minced parsley

1 tablespoon vegetable oil

1/3 cup chutney

1 tablespoon dry white wine or water

2 whole chicken breasts, cut into halves

12 ounces pea pods, cooked

Cook the orzo using the package directions; drain. Combine the orzo, parsley and oil in a bowl and toss to combine. Set aside and keep warm. Combine the chutney and wine in a saucepan. Cook until heated through. Remove from heat. Place the chicken skin side down in a broiling pan. Broil 5 to 6 inches from the heat source for 10 minutes on each side. Brush with the chutney mixture. Broil for an additional 5 minutes. Divide the orzo mixture among 4 plates. Arrange the pea pods over the orzo. Place 1 chicken breast half over the pea pods. Top with the remaining chutney mixture.

Yield: 4 servings

COMPANY'S BEST CHICKEN

2 (8-ounce) packages long grain wild rice mix

1/2 teaspoon salt

1/2 teaspoon pepper

12 skinless chicken breasts

1/2 cup butter

8 ounces mushrooms, sliced

1 tablespoon grated onion

2 cups whipping cream

1/4 cup dry sherry

Prepare the rice using the package directions. Spread over the bottom of a 9x13-inch baking dish. Sprinkle the salt and pepper over the chicken. Cook the chicken in the butter in a large skillet over low heat for 20 minutes. Remove the chicken and arrange over the rice. Add the mushrooms and onion to the drippings. Cook until tender, stirring frequently. Add the cream and sherry. Bring to a simmer. Simmer for 10 minutes. Pour over the chicken and rice. Bake at 350 degrees for 20 minutes.

Yield: 12 servings

FIREMAN'S CHICKEN POTPIE

3 boneless skinless chicken breasts, cooked, chopped

1 (8-ounce) can mixed vegetables, drained

1 (10-ounce) can cream of chicken soup

Salt and pepper to taste

2 all ready pie pastries

Combine the chicken and vegetables in a bowl and mix well. Add the soup, salt and pepper and mix well. Fit one of the pie pastries into a 9-inch pie plate. Spoon the chicken mixture into the pastry-lined pie plate. Top with the remaining pie pastry, sealing the edge and cutting vents. Bake at 350 degrees for 20 to 25 minutes or until browned.

Yield: 4 servings

GRAND CHICKEN AND ARTICHOKE CASSEROLE

4 pounds chicken breasts

1 cup butter

1/2 cup flour

3 1/2 cups milk

3 ounces Swiss cheese, shredded

2 ounces Cheddar cheese, shredded

2 teaspoons MSG

2 garlic cloves, crushed

1 teaspoon red pepper

1 (8-ounce) jar button mushrooms, drained

2 (14-ounce) cans artichoke hearts, drained, cut into halves

Combine the chicken breasts with water to cover in a saucepan. Bring to a boil. Reduce the heat. Simmer until chicken is cooked through; drain. Remove the meat from the bones and cut into small pieces. Melt the butter in a saucepan. Stir in the flour. Add the milk, whisking constantly. Stir in the Swiss and Cheddar cheeses, MSG, garlic and red pepper. Cook until bubbly, stirring constantly. Add the chicken, mushrooms and artichokes and mix well. Spoon into a greased 9x13-inch baking dish. Bake at 350 degrees for 30 minutes.

Yield: 10 servings

CHICKEN SAVANNAH

1 egg
1 1/2 cups bread crumbs
1/2 teaspoon garlic powder
1/4 teaspoon pepper
6 boneless skinless chicken breasts
1/4 cup margarine
12 small new red potatoes
1 (6-ounce) jar mushrooms, drained

1 (14-ounce) can artichoke hearts, drained, cut into quarters
1 (10-ounce) can cream of mushroom soup
2 cups sour cream
1/2 cup dry white wine
2 tablespoons tarragon
1/4 cup grated Parmesan cheese
Paprika to taste

Beat the egg in a shallow dish. Combine the bread crumbs, garlic powder and pepper in a shallow dish and mix well. Dip the chicken in the beaten egg. Dredge in the bread crumb mixture. Brown the chicken on both sides in the margarine in a skillet. Remove the chicken and place in a 9x13-inch baking dish. Arrange the potatoes, mushrooms and artichokes around the chicken. Add the soup, sour cream, wine and tarragon to the pan drippings and mix well. Pour over the chicken and vegetables. Sprinkle with the Parmesan cheese and paprika. Bake, covered, at 350 degrees for 45 minutes.

Yield: 6 servings

WILD TURKEY SAUCE

Combine 2 cups barbecue sauce, 3/4 cup packed brown sugar, 3/4 cup bourbon, such as Wild Turkey, 1 tablespoon minced onion and 1/2 cup water in a bowl and mix well. Pour over meatballs in a slow cooker. Cook on Low for 3 to 4 hours; do not remove the lid.

CHICKEN AND SPINACH PIZZA

Frozen bread dough and pizza sauce speed preparation of this hearty pizza.

2 tablespoons cornmeal
2 (1-pound) loaves frozen honey wheat bread dough, thawed
3 cups shredded mozzarella cheese
1 (16-ounce) package frozen chopped spinach, thawed, drained
1 egg, slightly beaten
2 teaspoons oregano
8 ounces Italian turkey sausage
1 cup chopped onion
1^1/$_2$ cups cubed cooked chicken
1 (8-ounce) jar pizza sauce
2 tablespoons butter, melted
^{1}/$_4$ cup grated Parmesan cheese

Sprinkle the cornmeal over the bottom of a greased 14-inch deep-dish pizza pan. Shape 1^1/$_4$ loaves of the bread dough into a ball. Roll into an 18-inch circle on a lightly floured surface. Fit into the pizza pan, pressing firmly against the bottom and sides. Sprinkle with 1^1/$_2$ cups of the mozzarella cheese. Shape the remaining bread dough into a ball. Roll into a 14-inch circle on a lightly floured surface. Combine the spinach, egg, remaining 1^1/$_2$ cups mozzarella cheese and oregano in a bowl and mix well. Cook the sausage with the onion in a skillet over medium heat until sausage is browned; drain. Stir in the chicken and pizza sauce. Layer the sausage mixture and the spinach mixture over the pizza dough. Place the 14-inch circle of dough over the layers. Pinch the edge of the dough to seal. Brush the top of the dough with the melted butter. Sprinkle with Parmesan cheese. Bake at 400 degrees for 20 to 25 minutes or until golden brown. Let stand for 10 minutes.

Yield: 8 servings

Chicken Enchiladas

1 (10-ounce) can cream of chicken soup
1 cup sour cream
3 to 4 cups cubed or shredded cooked chicken
1 (16-ounce) can refried beans
10 (6- to 8-inch) flour tortillas

3 cups shredded Cheddar cheese
1 (15-ounce) can enchilada sauce
$1/4$ cup sliced green onions
$1/4$ cup sliced black olives
$1/4$ cup sliced green olives
Spicy Black Bean Salsa

Combine the soup and sour cream in a bowl and mix well. Stir in the chicken. Spread 2 tablespoons of the beans over each tortilla. Spoon $1/3$ cup chicken mixture down center of each tortilla. Sprinkle with 1 tablespoon of the cheese. Roll each tortilla up and place seam side down in a greased 9x13-inch baking dish. Pour the enchilada sauce over the tortillas. Sprinkle with the green onions, black olives, green olives and remaining cheese. Bake at 350 degrees for 35 minutes. Serve with Spicy Black Bean Salsa. *Tip:* May substitute low-fat ingredients.

Yield: 4 to 6 servings

Spicy Black Bean Salsa

2 plum tomatoes, chopped
1 medium cucumber, seeded, chopped
1 avocado, chopped
$1/2$ cup chopped purple onion
1 (15-ounce) can black beans, drained, rinsed

3 tablespoons chopped fresh cilantro
2 tablespoons olive oil
3 tablespoons fresh lime juice
4 teaspoons red wine vinegar
$1/4$ teaspoon crushed red pepper
$1/4$ teaspoon garlic salt

Combine the tomatoes, cucumber, avocado, onion, beans and cilantro in a bowl and mix well. Combine the oil, lime juice, vinegar, red pepper and garlic salt in a bowl and mix well. Pour over the bean mixture and mix well. Refrigerate, covered, until completely chilled.

Yield: 3 to 4 cups

DUCK STROGANOFF

2 large onions	Salt and pepper to taste
4 cups chopped duck breast	Paprika to taste
1/4 cup butter	1 (6-ounce) can whole or sliced
6 tablespoons catsup	mushrooms
3 tablespoons soy sauce	2 cups sour cream
3/4 cup water	Cornstarch

Cut the onions into halves lengthwise and slice thinly. Sauté the duck in the butter in a skillet. Remove duck to a large saucepan. Sauté the onions in the pan drippings until tender. Add to the duck and mix well. Combine the catsup, soy sauce, water, salt, pepper and paprika in a bowl and mix well. Pour over the duck mixture. Bring to a simmer. Simmer for 1 1/2 hours or longer. Stir in the mushrooms and sour cream. Dissolve the cornstarch in a small amount of cold water in a cup. Pour into the duck mixture. Cook until thickened, stirring frequently. Serve over rice.

Yield: 10 servings

FORT MCALLISTER DUCK CASSEROLE

2 wild ducks	1/2 cup butter
1 onion, sliced	1/4 cup flour
2 ribs celery	1 1/2 cups light cream
1 (6-ounce) package long grain wild rice mix	1 tablespoon chopped parsley
8 ounces bulk hot sausage	1 1/2 teaspoons salt
1/2 onion, chopped	1/4 teaspoon pepper
8 ounces mushrooms, sliced	1 (2-ounce) package slivered almonds

Combine the ducks with enough water to cover in a stockpot. Add the sliced onion and celery ribs. Bring to a boil. Reduce the heat. Simmer until ducks are cooked through. Remove the ducks. Cut into small pieces, discarding the skin and bones. Place duck in a large bowl. Prepare the rice using the package directions. Add to the duck. Brown the sausage in a skillet, stirring until crumbly; drain. Add to the duck. Sauté the chopped onion and mushrooms in the butter in a skillet until tender. Stir in the flour. Add the cream, whisking constantly. Cook until thickened, stirring constantly. Add to the duck mixture. Add the parsley, salt and pepper and mix well. Spoon into a 2-quart baking dish. Sprinkle with the almonds. Bake at 350 degrees for 30 minutes.

Yield: 6 to 8 servings

STUFFED GEORGIA QUAIL

From Chandler Echols, Chef
Savannah Golf Club

6 quail	1/4 cup balsamic vinegar
1/4 cup Worcestershire sauce	1 teaspoon pepper
1/4 cup teriyaki sauce	1 teaspoon sugar
2 tablespoons chopped garlic	1 teaspoon chili powder
2 tablespoons chopped fresh rosemary	Peanut Stuffing
1/4 cup red wine	Olive oil to taste

Place the quail in a shallow dish. Combine the Worcestershire sauce, teriyaki sauce, garlic, rosemary, wine, vinegar, pepper, sugar and chili powder in a bowl and mix well. Pour over the quail. Marinate, covered, in the refrigerator for 3 hours, turning occasionally. Drain the quail. Stuff each quail with the Peanut Stuffing. Baste with a small amount of olive oil. Wrap a small amount of foil around the quail to hold it together. Place quail in a baking pan. Bake at 350 degrees for 15 to 20 minutes or until cooked through.

Yield: 6 servings

PEANUT STUFFING

1/2 onion, chopped	12 blackberries
1 red bell pepper, chopped	Salt to taste
1 rib celery, chopped	1 teaspoon oregano
3 tablespoons butter	1 egg, beaten
8 ounces sausage	6 slices white bread, torn into small pieces
1 cup boiled peanuts, shelled	

Sauté the onion, red pepper and celery in butter in a large skillet until tender. Cook the sausage in a skillet; drain. Add to the onion mixture. Stir in the peanuts and blackberries. Add the salt, oregano and egg and mix well. Fold in the bread and mix well.

BAKED DOVE

12 dove breasts or quail	1 cup sliced mushrooms
$^1/_2$ cup butter	1 yellow bell pepper, chopped
1 cup chopped celery	1 cup white wine
1 large Vidalia onion, chopped	2 tablespoons lemon juice

Brown the dove on both sides in butter in a skillet. Remove dove and place in a 9x13-inch baking pan. Add the celery, onion, mushrooms and yellow pepper to the skillet. Sauté until tender. Add the wine and lemon juice. Bring to a boil, stirring frequently. Pour over the dove. Bake, covered, at 350 degrees for 2 hours. Serve with wild rice.

Yield: 4 servings

On March 21 the Admiral [Dewey] and his party were given a luncheon by prominent Savannahians at the Yacht Club at mid-day. That afternoon there was a splendid military parade in Park Extension in honor of the admiral, which was reviewed by him and Gen. Miles and their staff. Col. A.R. Lawton, who commanded the First Georgia Regiment in the Spanish-American War, was in charge of the parade.

The famous Artillery Punch was reputed to have been served at the mid-day luncheon for Adm. Dewey at the Yacht Club though no mention was made of the fact in the account of the luncheon appearing in the Savannah newspapers. Just whether the admiral sampled this famous beverage is not known. In any event, however, he was unable to appear at the splendid banquet prepared and served in his honor at the DeSoto Hotel on Wednesday night, March 21, until 11 o'clock, at the end of the dinner. Upon receiving a beautiful silver vase, he responded in these well-chosen words:

"Mr. Mayor, ladies and gentlemen, I regret that I was unable to take part in the festivities of this occasion, but I rejoice that I am able to be with you and to receive the beautiful gift from your beautiful city. I prize it more as a gift of the city which is loved so much. There is another gift which I will take with me and it is the kindly Southern hospitality which has been extended to myself and my wife by the ladies and gentlemen of Savannah."

Excerpt from *Savannah News* article, Saturday, October 25, 1958

PINK HOUSE
MONTE CRISTO SANDWICH

In the 1950s this was a favorite lunch special at the Pink House.

1 (1-ounce) slice turkey breast	2 slices white bread
1 (1-ounce) slice Swiss cheese	Monte Cristo Batter
1 (1-ounce) slice ham	Confectioners' sugar to taste

Layer the turkey, cheese and ham between the bread slices. Cut the sandwich into quarters, using wooden picks to hold the sandwich quarters together. Coat the sandwich quarters in Monte Cristo Batter. Cook in 350-degree oil until golden brown. Remove the wooden picks. Place on a paper napkin. Sprinkle with confectioners' sugar. Serve hot with black raspberry jelly.

Yield: 1 sandwich

MONTE CRISTO BATTER

$1^1/_2$ cups flour	1 egg yolk, beaten
1 tablespoon baking powder	1 egg white, stiffly beaten
$1^1/_4$ cups water	

Sift the flour and baking powder together. Combine half the water and the egg yolk in a bowl and mix well. Add the flour mixture, mixing from the outside to the center of the bowl. Stir in the remaining water. Fold in the egg white.

Yield: Batter for 5 sandwiches

Spanish moss, found in trees, offered a shady haven for Savannahians out
for a picnic or stroll through the parks.
The plant is a bromeliad and a member of the pineapple family. It is not a
parasite and does not choke the tree as many believe. . . . The moss moves about
by simply letting go and floating off in a breeze.
Savannah: People, Place and Events, Ron Freeman, 1998

FROM

TYBEE TROUT

TO

SHRIMP HOLLANDAISE

THE SCARBOROUGH HOUSE

PARTIES AT THE SCARBOROUGH HOUSE

William and Julia Scarborough were two of Savannah's leading citizens in the early years of the nineteenth century. William, an entrepreneur of the first order, became known in financial circles as the "Merchant Prince." Julia also had a royal title thanks to her numerous and lavish parties. She was dubbed the "Countess."

The parties at the Scarboroughs' handsome home were the stuff of legend. One participant recounted,

> We hear ladies with families of small children boast of having been out to parties ten nights in succession until after midnight, and sometimes 3 o'clock in the morning; and that they had not seen their husbands for a week. . . . Mrs. Scarborough lately sent out cards of invitation to five hundred persons. Three hundred attended. Every room in the house was newly furnished for the occasion, the beds, etc. sent out; refreshments handed round from garret to cellar through the night.

The Scarboroughs' most famous fete took place to honor President James Monroe in May 1819. Monroe arrived in Savannah on board Scarborough's ship the S.S. *Savannah*, which became the first steamship to cross the Atlantic. After the President dedicated Independent Presbyterian Church, he attended a ball hosted by the Scarboroughs in their newly completed home that had been designed by architect John Jay. The city council appropriated five thousand dollars to help defray the cost. Not noted for his modesty, Scarborough described to his wife the pavilion he had Jay add to the house to accommodate the numerous guests:

> It is lined with red baize or flannel with festoons and pilasters of white muslin. It is also most tastefully and diligently done and by candle light will look most superbly. The President must be pleased with Savannah—as in the whole course of his extended tour, he may be received at a most costly and splendid rate, but no where with such pure and genuine taste.

Frank O. Braynard, *S.S. Savannah: The Elegant Steamship*. Athens: University of Georgia Press, 1963.

GRILLED MAHIMAHI AND CREAMY GRITS

8 mahimahi or firm fish of choice

2 tablespoons olive oil-based salad dressing

White pepper to taste

Freshly ground black pepper to taste

Salt to taste

Creamy Grits

Brush the fillets with salad dressing. Season with white pepper, black pepper and salt. Grill over hot coals for 4 minutes; turn. Grill for an additional 4 minutes or until fillets flake easily. Serve over Creamy Grits.

Yield: 8 servings

CREAMY GRITS

12 cups chicken broth

4 cups coarse stone-ground white grits

1 cup heavy cream

Salt to taste

Bring 11 cups of the broth to a boil in a saucepan. Add the grits slowly, stirring constantly. Reduce the heat, stirring constantly. Cook for 20 minutes, stirring frequently. Stir in the cream. Cook for an additional 10 minutes. Add remaining broth as needed for consistency. Season with salt.

"I care not who makes our Presidents as long as I can eat in Savannah."
Mark Hanna
Betsy Fancher—Book, *Savannah: A Renaissance of the Heart*

FLOUNDER FOLLY

1 large Vidalia onion,
cut into rings
4 tomatoes, peeled, cut into thick
slices
$1/2$ cup seasoned bread crumbs
$1/2$ cup grated Parmesan cheese

4 flounder fillets
Salt and pepper to taste
$1/4$ cup lemon juice
$1/4$ cup butter, melted
$1/2$ cup white wine
1 lemon, thinly sliced

Arrange the onion rings over the bottom of a greased 9x13-inch baking dish. Arrange the tomato slices over the onions. Sprinkle the bread crumbs and $1/4$ cup of the Parmesan cheese over the tomatoes. Place the fillets over the bread crumbs. Season with salt and pepper. Combine the lemon juice, butter and wine in a bowl and mix well. Pour over the layers. Sprinkle with the remaining $1/4$ cup Parmesan cheese. Arrange the lemon slices over the top. Bake at 325 degrees for 20 minutes or until fish flakes easily.

Yield: 4 servings

FLOUNDER STUFFED WITH CRAB MEAT

6 flounder fillets
1 pound crab meat
$3/4$ cup butter, melted

3 teaspoons oregano
Juice of 2 lemons

Fill the center of each fillet with an equal portion of the crab meat. Combine the butter, oregano and lemon juice in a bowl and mix well. Pour over the crab meat and fillets. Fold each end to the middle, covering the crab meat and overlapping the two ends. Secure with a wooden pick. Bake at 400 degrees for 40 minutes, basting with the juices occasionally.

Yield: 6 servings

ITALIAN FLOUNDER FILLETS

3 pounds flounder fillets
1/2 cup Italian salad dressing
1/2 cup mayonnaise

2 teaspoons grated onion
1/4 teaspoon Tabasco sauce
1 cup grated Parmesan cheese

Arrange the fillets in a single layer in a shallow dish. Pour the salad dressing over the fillets. Marinate in the refrigerator for 1 to 2 hours; drain. Combine the mayonnaise, onion, Tabasco sauce and Parmesan cheese in a bowl and mix well. Place the fillets on a rack in a broiler pan. Broil for 3 to 4 minutes. Top with the mayonnaise mixture. Broil for 4 minutes longer or until fillets flake easily. Serve with lemon slices.

Yield: 6 servings

BAKED SEA BASS WITH POTATOES

1/2 cup extra-virgin olive oil
2 large Idaho potatoes, peeled, cut into 1/8-inch thick slices
2 garlic cloves, finely chopped
1/2 teaspoon finely chopped fresh thyme leaves, or 1/4 teaspoon dried

Salt and pepper to taste
1 (2-pound) sea bass
3 tomatoes, peeled, seeded, coarsely chopped
15 brine-cured black olives, coarsely chopped

Coat the bottom of an oval baking dish with a small amount of olive oil. Layer the potatoes in the dish in an overlapping pattern, seasoning each layer with garlic, thyme, salt, pepper and a portion of the 1/2 cup olive oil. Bake for 20 minutes. Rinse the fish in cold water. Scrape off the scales using the back of a small knife. Rub the fish with a small amount of olive oil. Season with salt and pepper. Place the fish over the potatoes. Arrange the tomatoes and olives around the fish. Bake at 400 degrees for 30 minutes or until fish flakes easily with a fork.

Yield: 2 servings

PECAN-CRUSTED SEA BASS WITH SWEET POTATO BUTTER

From Bernard McDonough, Executive Chef
The Ford Plantation

4 (6- to 8-ounce) fresh sea bass fillets
Kosher salt to taste
Ground white pepper to taste
1/4 cup flour

1 egg, beaten
1/2 cup chopped pecans
1/4 cup clarified butter
1/2 cup dry white wine
Sweet Potato Butter

Season the fillets with kosher salt and pepper. Dip the fillets top side down in the flour, egg and then pecans. Sauté the fillets pecan side down in the clarified butter in an ovenproof skillet over medium heat for 2 to 3 minutes. Turn the fillets. Add the wine to the skillet. Bake at 350 degrees for 8 minutes or until fillets flake easily with a fork. Serve with Sweet Potato Butter.

Yield: 4 servings

SWEET POTATO BUTTER

1 sweet potato, peeled, chopped
2 shallots, chopped
1 cup fish stock
1 cup dry white wine

1/4 cup heavy cream
Dash of cayenne
Salt and black pepper to taste
1 tablespoon butter

Combine the sweet potato, shallots, stock and wine in a heavy saucepan and mix well. Cook over high heat until all the liquid has cooked off. Add the cream, cayenne, salt and black pepper. Bring to a boil. Reduce the heat. Add the butter slowly, whisking constantly. Purée in a blender container. Serve warm.

Twelve of us sat down to dinner, and on the sideboard were fourteen cut-glass decanters of the famous wine. I have never helped to eat a more sumptuous repast. I remember the terrapin soup, the soft-shelled crab, and particularly the little oyster crabs. Claret and champagne flowed like the water over Niagra Falls, but the Madeira wine remained in solitary and undisturbed state till dessert was served. Then the decanters began to move. The etiquette was for each man to attend to his neighbour's glass and only one man shirked his obligations.

Francis Richard, Earl of Warwick and Brooke, *Memories of Sixty Years*, 1917.

STEAMED SEA BASS WITH GINGER

1 (1 1/2- to 2-pound) sea bass
1 tablespoon vegetable oil
Salt to taste
1 teaspoon sugar

1 bunch scallions, cut into
2-inch pieces
1 tablespoon shredded gingerroot
8 ounces mushrooms
1 tablespoon sherry

Score both sides of the fish with diagonal slashes. Rinse and pat dry. Rub the fish with vegetable oil. Place the fish in a shallow pan. Sprinkle with salt and sugar. Arrange the scallions, gingerroot and mushrooms over the fish. Drizzle with sherry. Cover and steam for 15 minutes or until fish flakes easily.

Yield: 4 servings

PARTY SALMON STEAKS

These are easy to prepare. They can be fixed ahead and cooked at the last minute.

4 (1-inch thick) salmon steaks
2 lemons
Seasoning salt to taste
1/2 cup mayonnaise

Nutmeg to taste
1 cup sliced mushrooms
1/4 cup grated Parmesan cheese

Place the salmon steaks in a greased oblong baking dish. Squeeze the juice of 1/2 lemon over each steak. Sprinkle generously with the salt. Spread 2 tablespoons of the mayonnaise over each steak. Sprinkle lightly with the nutmeg. Arrange the mushrooms over the steaks. Sprinkle with the Parmesan cheese. Bake at 400 degrees for 15 minutes or until steaks flake easily.

Yield: 4 servings

WATERMELON FIRE AND ICE SALSA

Combine 3 cups seeded, chopped watermelon, 1/2 cup chopped green bell pepper,
2 tablespoons lime juice, 1 tablespoon chopped cilantro, 1 tablespoon chopped
green Vidalia onion and 1 to 2 chopped, seeded jalapeños in a bowl and mix
well. Refrigerate, covered, for 1 hour or longer.

Yield: 6 (1/2-cup) servings

THUNDERBOLT MARINATED SALMON

$^1/_2$ cup Provençal Herb-Scented Oil

$1^1/_2$ pounds frozen salmon fillet, thawed

20 black peppercorns, crushed

$^1/_2$ cup balsamic vinegar

2 teaspoons salt

1 tablespoon finely chopped chives

2 tablespoons small capers

Brush the bottoms of eight 10-inch plates with a small amount of the oil. Slice or pound the salmon fillet into $^1/_8$-inch thick slices. Arrange the slices over the bottom of the plates. Combine the peppercorns, vinegar and salt in a saucepan. Bring to a boil over medium heat. Boil until reduced to $^1/_4$ cup. Strain and let cool. Stir in the chives. Whisk in the remaining oil. Brush or lightly spoon over the salmon. Chill for 15 minutes. Sprinkle the capers over each plate. *Variation:* May substitute 3 tablespoons finely chopped fresh tarragon, chervil, parsley, dill, basil or fennel fronds combined with $^1/_2$ cup extra-virgin olive oil for the Provençal Herb-Scented Oil.

Yield: 8 servings

PROVENÇAL HERB-SCENTED OIL

20 (about) thyme sprigs

10 (about) marjoram sprigs

5 (about) oregano sprigs

20 (about) basil leaves

1 (1-quart) bottle extra-virgin olive oil with $^1/_2$ cup removed

Place the thyme, marjoram, oregano and basil in the olive oil bottle. Place the top on the bottle. Store at room temperature for 1 week and then store in the refrigerator.

Russo's Boneless Shad

1 (3-pound) boneless shad
1/4 cup lemon juice
1/2 cup butter, softened
1 teaspoon salt

1 teaspoon pepper
1 teaspoon paprika
Roe of 1 shad (optional)

Preheat the broiler. Place the shad flesh side up on greased foil in a broiling pan. Drizzle with the lemon juice. Spread the butter over the shad. Sprinkle with the salt, pepper and paprika. Place the roe next to the shad. Broil 10 inches from the heat source for 20 minutes, turning the roe once.

Yield: 6 servings

Baked Red Snapper

1 (3- to 4-pound) red snapper or other dressed fish
1 1/2 teaspoons salt

Sour Cream Dressing
2 tablespoons melted butter

Sprinkle the snapper with the salt. Stuff loosely with the Sour Cream Dressing. Close the opening with wooden picks. Place in a greased baking dish. Brush with the melted butter. Bake at 350 degrees for 40 to 60 minutes or until snapper flakes easily, basting occasionally. Remove wooden picks. Garnish with parsley and lemon or lime.

Yield: 6 servings

Sour Cream Dressing

3/4 cup chopped celery
1/2 cup chopped onion
1/4 cup melted butter or vegetable oil
1/2 cup sour cream
2 tablespoons grated lemon or lime peel

1 teaspoon paprika
1 teaspoon salt
1/4 cup chopped peeled lemon or lime
4 cups dry small bread cubes

Cook the celery and onion in the butter in a saucepan until tender. Add the sour cream, lemon peel, paprika, salt and lemon and mix well. Stir in the bread cubes.

MUSTARD-CRUSTED TROUT FILLET

6 ounces trout, red snapper
or bass fillet
Salt to taste
2 tablespoons light mayonnaise
1 tablespoon Dijon mustard

$^1/2$ cup fresh sourdough
bread crumbs
2 garlic cloves, minced
Paprika to taste (optional)
$^3/4$ teaspoon grated lemon peel

Place the fillet skin side down on a foil-lined 10x15-inch baking pan. Sprinkle with salt. Combine the mayonnaise and mustard in a bowl and mix well. Spread over the fillet. Combine the bread crumbs and garlic in a small bowl and mix well. Sprinkle over the fish, patting lightly. Sprinkle with paprika. Bake at 425 degrees for 20 minutes or until fish flakes easily and bread crumbs are golden brown. Sprinkle with lemon peel. Serve with lemon wedges.

Yield: 1 serving

TROUT DIJON

6 medium trout
Dijon mustard to taste

Salt and lemon pepper to taste
$^1/2$ cup butter

Rub the inside of the trout with mustard. Sprinkle with salt and lemon pepper. Melt the butter in a large skillet over medium heat. Add the trout. Cook for 4 minutes; turn. Cook an additional 4 minutes or until trout flakes easily. Serve with lemon wedges. *Variation:* Place trout in a foil-lined shallow baking pan. Add enough milk to bring to a $^1/4$-inch depth. Bake at 350 degrees for 20 minutes or until trout flakes easily.

Yield: 6 servings

TYBEE TROUT

4 fresh trout fillets or Spanish mackerel
2 teaspoons butter, melted
$^1/_4$ teaspoon paprika

$^1/_4$ teaspoon salt
$^1/_4$ teaspoon pepper
1 orange, peeled, sliced
Citrus Sauce

Preheat the broiler. Place the fillets on a greased rack in a broiler pan. Tuck under thin edges. Combine the butter, paprika, salt and pepper in a bowl and mix well. Brush over the fish. Arrange the orange slices around the fillets. Broil 4 inches from the heat source for 5 minutes or until fillets flake easily. Serve with Citrus Sauce.

Yield: 4 servings

CITRUS SAUCE

$^1/_2$ cup light sour cream
2 tablespoons orange marmalade

$^1/_4$ teaspoon thyme

Combine the sour cream, orange marmalade and thyme in a bowl and mix well. Chill.

The Crab Man's Call
"I'm talking 'bout devil' crabs—I'm talking 'bout devil' crab
***Datatatatatat, when I done—talking 'bout steam' crabs,
I'm talking 'bout devil' crabs."

. . . the cry is varied:
"I'm talking 'bout de pocketbook—I'm talking 'bout de pocketbook
***Datatatatat, when I done—talking 'bout de pocketbook
I'm talking 'bout devil' crabs."

Excerpt from *Savannah News* article:
"Street Calls of the South"

Marie Smith's Seafood Casserole

This is a fabulous dish. It can be either very expensive or not, depending upon whether you catch your own seafood.

$^1/_2$ cup milk

1 cup mayonnaise

1 cup tomato juice

1 egg, beaten

2 cups cooked rice

$^1/_2$ cup chopped onion

$^1/_2$ cup chopped green bell pepper

1 cup chopped celery

1 (3-ounce) can sliced mushrooms

$1^1/_2$ pounds shrimp, chopped

1 pound crab meat

Salt and pepper to taste

Bread crumbs to taste

Slivered almonds to taste

Mix the milk, mayonnaise, tomato juice and egg in a bowl. Stir in the rice, onion, green pepper, celery, mushrooms, shrimp and crab meat. Season with salt and pepper. Spoon into a greased 3-quart baking dish. Sprinkle with bread crumbs and almonds. Bake at 350 degrees for 45 minutes.

Yield: 8 to 10 servings

Ultimate Seafood

$2^1/_2$ pounds shrimp

Salt and pepper to taste

2 tablespoons butter

2 tablespoons flour

2 cups heavy cream

$^1/_2$ teaspoon mustard

$^1/_2$ teaspoon curry powder

$^1/_2$ teaspoon paprika

1 tablespoon Worcestershire sauce

1 tablespoon catsup

2 tablespoons sherry

2 tablespoons lemon juice

2 (14-ounce) cans artichoke hearts, cut into halves

1 pound crab meat

Paprika to taste

$1^1/_2$ cups shredded Cheddar cheese

Combine the shrimp with enough water to cover in a saucepan. Bring to a boil. Reduce the heat. Simmer until shrimp turn pink; drain and peel. Season with salt and pepper. Set aside. Melt the butter in a separate saucepan. Stir in the flour. Add the cream, whisking constantly. Whisk in the mustard, curry, $^1/_2$ teaspoon paprika, Worcestershire sauce, catsup, sherry and lemon juice. Cook until sauce thickens. Layer the artichoke hearts, crab meat and shrimp in a shallow baking dish. Pour the sauce over the layers. Sprinkle with paprika and cheese. Bake at 375 degrees for 20 minutes.

Yield: 10 servings

CREPES OF CRAB MEAT BERCY

2 tablespoons butter
8 ounces mushrooms, sliced
2 tablespoons lemon juice
1 tablespoon minced
green onions
$1/4$ cup dry sherry
2 (8-ounce) bottles clam juice
$1/4$ teaspoon salt

Dash of cayenne
2 tablespoons chopped parsley
$1/2$ cup melted butter
$1/4$ cup flour
1 pound crab meat
16 crepes (page 136)
3 tablespoons bread crumbs

Preheat the broiler. Melt the 2 tablespoons butter in a skillet. Add the mushrooms. Sprinkle with the lemon juice. Cook for 5 minutes. Add the green onions. Cook for 1 minute. Add the sherry, clam juice, salt, cayenne and parsley and mix well. Bring to a boil. Reduce the heat. Simmer for 2 minutes. Combine $1/4$ cup of the melted butter and the flour in a small bowl and mix well. Stir into the mushroom mixture. Cook until mixture thickens. Stir in the crab meat. Simmer for 5 minutes or until crab meat is heated through. Place 3 tablespoons of the crab mixture on each crepe and roll up. Arrange crepes on an ovenproof platter. Sprinkle with bread crumbs. Drizzle with the remaining $1/4$ cup melted butter. Broil until golden brown.

Yield: 8 servings

The truck farmers of the South, who drive into the cities on the market days of each week
(Tuesday, Friday, and Saturday), also take a turn through the residential sections.
If their load consists of tomatoes, here is their slogan:

Tomato——o-o-o-o-oes
He's fresh——he's fine
Just off the vine
Tomato-o-o-o-o-oes

Excerpt from *Savannah News* Article: "Street Calls of the South"

CRAB CASSEROLE

1 pound claw or white crab meat
2 cups herb-seasoned stuffing mix
1 large onion, finely chopped
1 or 2 ribs celery, finely chopped

Salt and pepper to taste
$^1/_2$ cup butter or margarine, melted
2 cups half-and-half

Combine the crab meat, stuffing mix, onion, celery, salt and pepper in a bowl and mix well. Add the butter and half-and-half and stir to blend. Spoon into a greased 8x8-inch baking dish. Bake at 350 degrees for 30 to 40 minutes or until bubbly.

Yield: 4 servings

EDISTO CRAB CASSEROLE

5 eggs
$^1/_2$ cup mayonnaise
Juice of 1 lemon
Dash of hot sauce
Worcestershire sauce to taste
2 tablespoons Durkee sauce
1 cup sour cream

$^1/_2$ cup butter, melted
Salt and pepper to taste
2 pounds crab meat
7 slices toasted bread, torn into pieces
1 medium onion, grated

Combine the eggs, mayonnaise, lemon juice, hot sauce, Worcestershire sauce, Durkee sauce, sour cream, butter, salt and pepper in a bowl and mix well. Stir in the crab meat, bread and onion and mix well. Spoon into a greased 2-quart baking dish. Bake at 325 degrees for 35 minutes or until golden brown.

Yield: 8 servings

A shrimp seller invites his customers out, not presuming as one may imagine,
to step within their kitchens. At any rate, he cries:

Fresh shrimps—fresh shrimps.
If you want to see me.
Come down with the dishpan,
Come down with the dishpan,
Fresh shrimps—fresh shrimps.

Excerpt from *Savannah News* Article: "Street Calls of the South"

MOON RIVER CRAB CAKES

They are best made with fresh crab meat.

3 scallions	1 teaspoon Worcestershire sauce
1 teaspoon butter	1 pound crab meat
1/4 cup chopped green bell pepper	Salt to taste
	Cayenne to taste
1/4 cup chopped celery	1 cup fine bread crumbs
2/3 cup mayonnaise	3 tablespoons vegetable oil
1 egg, lightly beaten	

Chop the scallions, reserving the tops for garnish. Sauté the scallions in butter in a skillet until tender; cool. Combine the cooked scallions, green pepper, celery, mayonnaise, egg and Worcestershire sauce in a bowl and mix well. Fold in the crab meat. Season with salt and cayenne. Stir in enough of the bread crumbs to hold the mixture together. Shape into small patties. Cook in hot oil in a skillet until browned, turning once. Remove from the skillet and place on baking sheets. Bake at 350 degrees for 10 minutes. Serve with Creamy Dijon Sauce. *Tip:* May be refrigerated after cooking in oil and baked before serving.

Yield: 4 to 6 servings

CREAMY DIJON SAUCE

2 tablespoons water	1 cup mayonnaise
1 tablespoon sugar	2 tablespoons white vinegar
1/2 cup whipping cream	2 tablespoons Dijon mustard

Combine the water and sugar in a saucepan and mix well. Heat until the sugar dissolves; cool. Beat the cream in a mixer bowl until soft peaks form. Combine the mayonnaise, vinegar, mustard and cooled sugar mixture in a bowl and blend well. Fold in the whipped cream.

Yield: 4 servings

POTATO ISLAND DEVILED CRAB

1/2 onion, chopped
1/2 green bell pepper, chopped
2 ribs celery, chopped
1/4 cup bacon drippings or butter
1/2 cup catsup
2 tablespoons mayonnaise
1 tablespoon mustard
2 eggs, slightly beaten
2 tablespoons Worcestershire sauce
1 cup crushed butter crackers
1 pound crab meat
1/4 cup butter, melted
1/2 cup cornflakes

Sauté the onion, green pepper and celery in the bacon drippings in a skillet until tender. Combine with the catsup, mayonnaise, mustard, eggs, Worcestershire sauce and crushed crackers in a bowl and mix well. Stir in the crab meat. Spoon into a greased baking dish. Combine the melted butter and cornflakes in a bowl and mix well. Sprinkle over the crab mixture. Bake at 350 degrees for 20 to 30 minutes or until bubbly. *Variation:* Boil crab shells in water to cover with a small amount of dish detergent for 10 minutes. Clean thoroughly. Spoon the crab mixture into the shells and place on a baking sheet. Bake for 20 to 30 minutes.

Yield: 4 servings

BAKED OYSTERS SAVANNAH

1 pint oysters
1 garlic clove
1/4 cup butter
8 ounces mushrooms, sliced
1/2 cup bread crumbs
Salt and pepper to taste
3 slices bacon, cut into 1-inch pieces

Divide the oysters among 4 ramekins. Sauté the garlic in 2 tablespoons of the butter in a skillet. Remove the garlic and discard. Add the mushrooms to the skillet. Sauté the mushrooms until tender. Place 1/4 of the mushrooms in each ramekin with the oysters. Add the remaining 2 tablespoons butter to the skillet. Stir in the bread crumbs. Season with salt and pepper. Sprinkle the bread crumb mixture over the oysters and mushrooms. Arrange the bacon pieces over the bread crumbs. Bake at 450 degrees for 10 to 15 minutes or until the bacon is crisp.

Yield: 4 servings

Carnival Loaf

Ideal for a Mardi Gras buffet or a casual get-together. A picture-perfect stuffed oyster and spinach loaf can be prepared hours in advance, stored in the refrigerator, and popped in the oven about 45 minutes before serving.

1 (10-ounce) package frozen chopped spinach

$1/4$ cup olive oil

4 tablespoons butter, softened

1 garlic clove, minced

1 (10-inch round) Vienna, Italian or homemade bread loaf

3 eggs

$3/4$ cup mayonnaise

6 slices bacon, cooked, crumbled

Pinch of mace

Salt and freshly ground pepper to taste

1 pint medium oysters

2 medium tomatoes, sliced

$1/2$ cup grated Parmesan cheese

Cook the spinach in a saucepan using the package directions and adding the olive oil to the water; drain. Cream the butter and garlic in a mixer bowl until light and fluffy. Set aside. Slice off the top of the bread loaf. Scoop out the center, leaving a $1/2$-inch shell. Process the bread in a blender to make small bread crumbs. Whisk the eggs with the mayonnaise in a bowl. Stir in the bacon, cooked spinach, mace, salt and pepper. Spread the inside and the top of the loaf with the garlic butter. Drain the oysters and pat dry. Arrange the oysters over the bottom of the bread loaf. Layer the spinach mixture, tomato slices, bread crumbs and cheese $1/2$ at a time over the oysters. Replace the top of the bread loaf. Wrap in foil. Bake at 350 degrees for 45 minutes. Cut into 6 wedges. Garnish with parsley.

Yield: 6 servings

In 1791, George Washington was lavishly entertained by a thriving community of nearly 2,500.
Pg. 51, Excerpts from Edward Chang Sieg, *Eden on the Marsh: An Illustrated History of Savannah, 1985.* Windsor Publications.

DADDY BUB'S OYSTER PIE

1/2 cup evaporated milk	8 ounces saltine crackers
1/2 cup water	4 ribs celery, chopped
1/4 cup butter	8 ounces sharp cheese, sliced
1 quart large oysters, drained	Salt and pepper to taste

Combine the evaporated milk, water and butter in a saucepan. Bring to a boil; remove from heat immediately. Place the oysters in the milk mixture. Let stand for 5 minutes or longer. Drain, reserving the liquid. Layer 8 crushed crackers, celery, 4 cheese slices and drained oysters over the bottom of a 2-quart baking dish until all ingredients are used, ending with crackers and cheese. Sprinkle with salt and pepper. Pour enough of the reserved liquid over the layers to saturate the layers. Bake at 400 degrees for 10 minutes or until bubbly. Move to the top rack of the oven. Bake until browned.

Yield: 6 servings

OYSTERS FLORENTINE PARMIGIANA

24 shucked oysters with the liquor and deep shells	1 tablespoon Pernod
1 pound fresh spinach, or 1 (10-ounce) package frozen	1 1/2 teaspoons Worcestershire sauce
1/2 cup butter	1/2 cup fresh bread crumbs
1/2 cup chopped parsley	Dash of Tabasco sauce
2 chopped anchovy fillets	Salt and pepper to taste
	1 cup grated Parmesan cheese

Drain the oysters, reserving the liquid. Strain the liquid. Set the oysters aside in the shells. Bring a small amount of water to a boil in a saucepan. Add the spinach. Cook until tender; drain. Chop the spinach. Melt the butter in a saucepan. Stir in the cooked spinach, parsley and anchovy fillets. Stir in the Pernod, Worcestershire sauce and bread crumbs gradually. Purée coarsely in a blender, adding the reserved liquid as needed. Season with Tabasco sauce, salt and pepper. Place the oysters in the shell on a baking sheet. Place a spoonful of the puréed mixture over the oysters. Sprinkle with the cheese. Bake at 450 degrees for 5 to 10 minutes or until the cheese is melted and light brown.

Yield: 4 servings

THE BEST FRENCH-FRIED SHRIMP

*In the early summer when the shrimp that are caught in the May River are small, all we do
is head the shrimp and cook them with shells and tails. Excellent for a summer party.*

1 cup flour	1 cup ice water
1/2 teaspoon sugar	1 egg
1/2 teaspoon salt	2 pounds shrimp
2 tablespoons vegetable oil	

Combine the flour, sugar, salt, oil, ice water and egg in a bowl and mix well. Dip the shrimp in the
batter to coat. Cook 8 to 10 shrimp at a time in 350-degree oil. Drain on paper towels.

Yield: 8 servings

DAUFUSKIE ISLAND SHRIMP CREOLE

4 green onions or 1 Vidalia onion, chopped	2 teaspoons dried parsley
1/2 cup chopped celery	1/4 teaspoon cayenne
3/4 cup chopped green bell pepper	2 teaspoons Worcestershire sauce
1 garlic clove, minced	2 teaspoons soy sauce
2 tablespoons butter or margarine	1 teaspoon hot sauce
1 (16-ounce) can whole tomatoes or 4 fresh tomatoes, chopped	1 tablespoon lemon juice
1 (16-ounce) can tomato sauce	2 teaspoons curry powder (optional)
1 teaspoon salt	3 bay leaves (optional)
	1 cup golden raisins (optional)
	1 pound shrimp, peeled

Sauté the green onions, celery, green pepper and garlic in butter in a large saucepan until the green
onions are transparent. Add the tomatoes, tomato sauce, salt, parsley, cayenne, Worcestershire sauce,
soy sauce, hot sauce, lemon juice, curry powder, bay leaves and raisins and mix well. Bring to a
simmer. Simmer for 30 minutes. Add the shrimp. Cook over medium-low heat until the shrimp turn
pink. Remove the bay leaves. Serve over rice.

Yield: 4 to 6 servings

Georgia Bulldog Shrimp and Green Noodles

8 ounces spinach noodles

2 pounds shrimp, peeled, deveined

2 tablespoons butter

1 (10-ounce) can cream of mushroom soup

1 teaspoon Dijon mustard

1 cup mayonnaise

1 tablespoon chopped chives

$1/4$ cup dry sherry

1 cup sour cream

1 cup shredded Cheddar cheese

Cook the noodles using the package directions; drain. Line a 2-quart baking dish with the noodles. Sauté the shrimp in the butter in a skillet for 5 minutes or until the shrimp turn pink. Arrange the shrimp over the noodles. Pour half of the liquid from the skillet over the shrimp. Combine the soup, mustard, mayonnaise, chives, sherry, sour cream and $1/2$ cup of the cheese in a bowl and mix well. Pour over the shrimp. Bake at 350 degrees for 20 minutes. Sprinkle the remaining $1/2$ cup cheese over the top. Bake for an additional 10 minutes or until bubbly.

Yield: 10 servings

Garlic Shrimp with Pea Pods

8 ounces linguini

1 pound medium shrimp, peeled, deveined, cooked

8 ounces pea pods

1 cup roasted garlic salad dressing

Cook the linguini using the package directions. Add the shrimp and pea pods during the last 2 minutes of cooking time; drain. Combine the cooked linguini, shrimp, pea pods and dressing in a large bowl; toss to coat. Serve hot or cold. *Variation:* Marinate the shrimp in $1/2$ cup roasted garlic salad dressing for 1 hour before cooking.

Yield: 4 servings

HUSH PUPPIES

Mix 1 cup self-rising cornmeal, $1/2$ cup self-rising flour, 1 teaspoon sugar, $1/2$ teaspoon baking soda and 1 chopped onion in a bowl. Add enough buttermilk to make a slightly thick batter. Drop by teaspoonfuls into hot vegetable oil in a skillet. Cook until browned.

Yield: 8 servings

CREPES WITH SHRIMP IN TARRAGON

2¹/2 pounds shrimp, peeled, deveined
2 tablespoons butter
1 tablespoon chopped green onions
1 cup white wine
1 teaspoon salt

Dash of cayenne
3 tablespoons flour
3 tablespoons melted butter
1/2 teaspoon tarragon
2¹/2 cups cream or half-and-half
16 crepes

Cook the shrimp in the 2 tablespoons butter in a saucepan for 3 minutes or until pink. Add the green onions. Cook for 1 minute. Add the wine, salt and cayenne. Bring to a boil. Reduce the heat. Simmer for 2 to 3 minutes. Remove the shrimp with a slotted spoon; set aside. Combine the flour and melted butter in a small bowl. Add the tarragon and cream to the wine mixture. Bring to a boil. Stir in the flour mixture. Cook over medium heat until mixture is thickened, stirring constantly. Remove 1 cup of the sauce and keep warm. Set aside 8 shrimp for garnish. Chop the remaining shrimp. Add to the sauce. Bring to a boil. Remove from heat. Spoon 3 tablespoons of the shrimp mixture on each crepe and roll up. Place filled crepes on a platter. Spoon the reserved sauce over the crepes. Garnish with reserved shrimp.

Yield: 8 servings

CREPES

1 cup flour
1/4 teaspoon salt
3 eggs, beaten

1¹/4 cups milk
2 tablespoons melted butter or margarine

Sift the flour and salt in a bowl. Combine the eggs, milk and butter in a bowl and blend well. Pour into the flour mixture and mix well. Place 2 tablespoons of the batter in a greased 6- to 7-inch skillet. Tilt the skillet to coat the bottom. Cook over medium heat until lightly browned. Turn and cook the other side. Repeat with remaining batter. Refrigerate with sheets of waxed paper between the crepes and wrapped tightly in foil or plastic wrap for up to 2 weeks.

Yield: 24 crepes

IRRESISTIBLE CITRUS SHRIMP

Sweetness and a touch of spice give this shrimp dish irresistible flavor.

6 tablespoons butter
1/4 cup chopped green onions
3/4 teaspoon cumin
1/4 teaspoon red pepper sauce
1 pound medium shrimp, peeled, deveined
Juice of 1 medium orange

Juice of 1 lime
Zest of 1 lime
Zest of 1 medium orange
1/4 cup chopped fresh cilantro
1/4 teaspoon salt
8 ounces fettuccini, cooked, hot

Melt 2 tablespoons of the butter in a skillet until sizzling. Add the green onions, cumin and red pepper sauce. Cook over medium-high heat for 1 to 2 minutes or until green onions are tender. Add the shrimp. Cook for 2 to 3 minutes or until shrimp turn pink. Remove the shrimp. Increase the heat to high. Add the orange juice and 2 tablespoons of the lime juice. Cook for 4 to 5 minutes or until liquid is reduced to 1/3 cup. Remove from heat. Stir in the remaining 4 tablespoons butter 1 tablespoon at a time. Stir in the lime zest, orange zest, cilantro and salt. Add the shrimp, stirring to coat. Divide the fettuccini among 4 plates. Spoon the shrimp mixture over the fettuccini.

Yield: 4 servings

SHRIMP AND SPINACH CASSEROLE

4 (10-ounce) packages frozen chopped spinach, thawed, well drained
3 pounds medium shrimp, deveined, cooked
1/2 cup butter
1/2 cup flour
3 cups milk

1/2 cup chopped scallions
Salt and pepper to taste
Pinch of dry mustard
Pinch of nutmeg
1 cup dry white wine
2 cups shredded sharp Cheddar cheese
Paprika to taste

Arrange the spinach over the bottom of a 4-quart baking dish. Place the shrimp over the spinach. Melt the butter in a saucepan. Stir in the flour. Add the milk gradually, whisking constantly. Cook until mixture is smooth and thickened. Add the scallions, salt, pepper, mustard and nutmeg. Stir in the wine. Pour the mixture over the shrimp. Sprinkle with the cheese and paprika. Bake at 350 degrees for 35 minutes.

Yield: 6 servings

SHRIMP HOLLANDAISE

This dish has been very popular in the catering business. One of the benefits is that it tastes great piping hot or at room temperature.

4 cups water	1 medium onion, chopped
1 tablespoon salt	8 ounces mushrooms, sliced
1 teaspoon pepper	Butter
1 lemon, sliced	Blender Hollandaise Sauce
1 pound shrimp	Chopped fresh parsley
1^1/$_2$ cups rice	

Combine the water, salt, pepper and lemon slices in a large saucepan. Bring to a boil. Add the shrimp. Cook until shrimp turn pink. Remove the shrimp. Cook the liquid over high heat until reduced to 2 cups. Peel the shrimp. Add the rice and onion to the reduced liquid. Boil, covered, for 5 minutes. Reduce the heat to low. Cook for 20 minutes or until the rice is tender. Sauté the mushrooms in a small amount of butter in a skillet until tender. Layer the cooked rice mixture, sautéed mushrooms, cooked shrimp, Blender Hollandaise Sauce and parsley on a serving platter until all ingredients are used. *Tip:* Increase the ingredient amounts, making additional layers to serve any number of people.

Yield: 4 servings

BLENDER HOLLANDAISE SAUCE

3 egg yolks	2 dashes of hot sauce
Juice of 1 lemon	1 cup butter, melted
1 teaspoon salt	

Combine the egg yolks, lemon juice, salt and hot sauce in a blender container. Process at high speed, adding the butter in a thin stream.

In the old days, Savannah housekeepers bought either from the city market . . . , but more often from Negro vendors who plied the streets, carrying on their heads great baskets of shrimp, crabs and oysters, and filling the morning air with lyrical Geechee cries of
"Crab buy 'er! Yeh Swimps! Hey Oshta!"

Betsy Fancher—Book, *Savannah: A Renaissance of the Heart*

Shrimp and Vidalias in White Wine Marinade

1 pound shrimp, peeled, deveined
2 Vidalia onions
2 carrots, chopped
2 ribs celery, chopped, or
1/2 cup chopped broccoli
1 green bell pepper, chopped

6 tablespoons chablis or other white wine
1/4 cup lime juice
1 tablespoon olive oil
1 tablespoon sugar
1 teaspoon basil
1/2 teaspoon salt

Steam the shrimp until they turn pink. Slice the onions and separate into rings. Combine the shrimp, onion rings, carrots, celery and green pepper in a bowl and mix well. Whisk the chablis, lime juice, olive oil, sugar, basil and salt in a separate bowl. Pour over the shrimp mixture. Marinate, covered, in the refrigerator for 2 to 3 hours; drain. Serve over spinach leaves.

Yield: 4 servings

Skidaway Grilled Shrimp in Bacon

1 head radicchio
1 head endive
1 head Bibb lettuce
3 red or yellow bell peppers, julienned
20 medium shrimp, peeled, deveined

10 slices bacon, cut into halves
1/4 cup extra-virgin olive oil
2 tablespoons balsamic vinegar
1 tablespoon Pommery mustard
1 sprig of thyme

Wash and dry the radicchio, endive and Bibb lettuce. Tear into bite-size pieces. Place in a large bowl. Add the red peppers. Wrap each shrimp tightly in 1/2 slice of bacon. Grill on a rack over hot coals for 3 to 5 minutes or until crisp, turning once. Keep warm. Combine the oil, vinegar, mustard and thyme in a jar. Cover and shake well. Add the shrimp to the red peppers and greens. Pour the olive oil mixture over the shrimp mixture. Toss to coat. *Tip:* Shrimp may be cooked in a skillet.

Yield: 4 servings

WILMINGTON RIVER BARBECUED SHRIMP

3 pounds large shrimp
3 cups butter
3 tablespoons black pepper
1 teaspoon cayenne
1 teaspoon MSG

$1/2$ teaspoon paprika
$1/8$ teaspoon each rosemary, thyme and oregano
Pinch of cinnamon
2 teaspoons salt

Wash and drain the shrimp well. Place in a 7x11-inch microwave-safe baking dish. Combine the butter, black pepper, cayenne, MSG, paprika, rosemary, thyme, oregano and cinnamon in a microwave-safe bowl. Microwave on High for $1^1/2$ to 2 minutes or until butter is melted; mix well. Pour over shrimp. Microwave shrimp mixture, covered, on High for 10 to 12 minutes or until shrimp turn pink, stirring twice. Sprinkle with the salt. Let stand for 3 minutes. Serve with French bread.

Yield: 4 to 6 servings

SHRIMP CASSEROLE

2 tomatoes
8 ounces mushrooms, sliced
1 onion, minced
2 tablespoons butter
3 tablespoons flour
$1/2$ cup half-and-half

$1/2$ cup sherry
1 tablespoon Worcestershire sauce
3 pounds shrimp, cooked
Salt and pepper to taste
$1/2$ cup fresh buttered bread crumbs

Cut the tomatoes into quarters. Remove the seeds and juice. Sauté the mushrooms and onion in butter in a skillet until tender. Add the flour. Cook until browned, stirring constantly. Add the half-and-half, sherry, Worcestershire sauce, tomatoes, shrimp, salt and pepper. Cook until thickened, stirring constantly. Spoon into a 2-quart baking dish. Sprinkle the bread crumbs over the mixture. Bake at 350 degrees for 20 minutes.

Yield: 8 to 10 servings

Were you there when the Nancy Hanks made the mile-a-minute trip to Atlanta, and the Steamer St. Nicholas used to take picnic crowds to Tybee and land at the old wharf, where the tram cars would carry you to the beach?

FROM

PECAN PIE

TO

BOURBON
BROWNIES

PIES AND COOKIES

THE CATHEDRAL OF ST. JOHN THE BAPTIST

A COLONIAL WEDDING

William Stephens was sent by Georgia's Trustees to serve as the secretary for the colony from 1737 to 1750. During his tenure he meticulously kept a journal describing various events in the life of England's youngest colony.

In August of 1744, Stephens helped with the wedding of two of Savannah's more colorful citizens, Thomas Bosomworth, an adventurer/minister who for a while served as Secretary of Indian Affairs, and Mary Musgrove, a half Creek Indian, who was General James Oglethorpe's interpreter.

The wedding was quite an event, because Bosomworth invited most of his congregation (about sixty people) to the festivities. Stephens let the couple hold the festivities in the Trustees house, where he was living. He wrote in his journal:

I delivered the front rooms to their use, wherein rough Boards and Tressels, the Workmen made three long tables, and forms to Sit on, each Table. . . covered with a Cold repast of all such kind of provisions as this place could afford, boyled, Roasted and Baked, brought ready dressed. The Company met about 7, and the Tables were all filled when good Wine was not wanting to make Supper Compleat; and after that the Men and Women Separated a while when such as were most inclined to Tippling, were plentifully Supplied with a Small Beveridge, scarcely deserving the name of punch, but well Judged most proper for this hot Season, and probably was the means of not one Persons being disordered with Drink.

The festivities were not limited to eating and imbibing. After supper,

Dancing likewise was one ingredient in Merry Making, for which a Fiddle was prepared; and they that were disposed to such Exercise, found themselves partners 8 or 10 Couple at a time. In short nothing happen'd in the whole Company (large as it was) that gave any offence, everybody taking their own time to go home when they pleased; but the Dancers kept the latest hours, as tis rarely seen otherwise.

William Stephens. *The Journal of William Stephens, 1743–1745.* Ed. By E. Merton Coulter. Athens: University of Georgia Press, 1959.

DEEP-DISH APPLE CIDER PIE

1 cup apple cider	2 tablespoons lemon juice
$1/2$ cup sugar	$1/2$ teaspoon cinnamon
6 Granny Smith apples, thinly sliced	2 tablespoons cornstarch
$1^1/2$ cups raisins	1 baked (9-inch) deep-dish pie shell
1 teaspoon grated lemon peel	Pecan Topping

Combine the cider and sugar in a large saucepan. Bring to a boil. Stir in the apples, raisins, lemon peel, lemon juice and cinnamon. Simmer until apples are tender, stirring frequently. Dissolve the cornstarch in a small amount of water in a bowl. Stir into the apple mixture. Cook until mixture thickens, stirring constantly. Spoon into the pie shell. Sprinkle the Pecan Topping over the hot apple mixture. Bake at 400 degrees for 30 minutes or until golden brown. *Tip:* Using a food processor to slice the apples greatly reduces the preparation time.

Yield: 6 to 8 servings

PECAN TOPPING

$1/2$ cup packed brown sugar	$1/4$ cup butter
$1/2$ cup flour	1 cup pecans

Combine the brown sugar, flour, butter and pecans in a food processor container. Process until mixture resembles coarse crumbs.

Laurel Grove Cemetery—When the cemetery opened, it became quite fashionable to citizens to ride out on Sundays to visit not only the departed, but each other. With this in mind, Laurel Grove was laid out with green spaces and widelanes for carriages.

Savannah: People, Places and Events, Ron Freeman. 1998.

Binoffi Pie

The recipe for this wonderful dessert is from the Kinsale area of Ireland, where it is a favorite.

1 (14-ounce) can sweetened condensed milk

24 to 26 graham crackers, vanilla wafers or pecan sandies, crushed

1/4 cup butter, melted

2 to 3 bananas, sliced

2 cups whipping cream

Pour the condensed milk into a pie plate. Cover with foil and place in hot water. Bake at 425 degrees for 1 hour or until thick and caramel colored. Combine the graham cracker crumbs and melted butter in a 9-inch pie plate and mix well. Press over the bottom and up the side of the pie plate. Pour the cooked milk over the pie crust. Arrange the banana slices over the milk. Beat the cream in a mixer bowl until stiff peaks form. Spoon over the bananas. Refrigerate until ready to serve. *Tip:* This could be prepared in a rectangular pan and served as squares or in individual pastry cups.

Yield: 6 to 8 servings

Plantation Sour Cream Pie

1 cup sugar

1 tablespoon flour

1 cup sour cream

1 teaspoon nutmeg

1 teaspoon cinnamon

3 egg yolks

1/2 cup broken nuts

1 cup raisins

1 baked (9-inch) pie shell

3 egg whites

1/4 teaspoon cream of tartar

6 tablespoons sugar

Combine the 1 cup sugar, flour, sour cream, nutmeg, cinnamon and 3 egg yolks in a saucepan and mix well. Stir in the nuts and raisins. Cook until mixture thickens, stirring constantly. Spoon into the pie shell. Beat the 3 egg whites in a mixer bowl until foamy. Add the cream of tartar. Beat at high speed until soft peaks form. Add the 6 tablespoons sugar 1 tablespoon at a time, beating constantly at medium speed until blended. Beat at high speed until stiff and glossy. Spread over the hot filling, sealing to edge. Bake at 450 degrees or until meringue begins to brown.

Yield: 6 to 8 servings

FANNY'S HONEY-CRUNCH PECAN PIE

$1^1/3$ cups flour
1 teaspoon salt
$1/2$ cup butter-flavor shortening
3 to 4 tablespoons cold water
4 eggs, slightly beaten
1 cup light corn syrup
$1/4$ cup packed brown sugar

$1/4$ cup sugar
2 tablespoons butter or margarine, melted
1 tablespoon bourbon whiskey (optional)
1 teaspoon vanilla extract
1 cup chopped pecans
Crunch Topping

Preheat oven to 350 degrees. Combine the flour and $1/2$ teaspoon of the salt in a bowl. Cut in the shortening until crumbly. Add the water 1 tablespoon at a time, mixing with a fork until the mixture forms a ball. Roll into a 12-inch circle on a lightly floured surface. Fit into a 9-inch pie plate and flute the edge. Combine the eggs, corn syrup, brown sugar, sugar, butter, whiskey, vanilla and remaining $1/2$ teaspoon salt in a bowl and mix well. Stir in the pecans. Spoon into the pie pastry. Bake for 40 minutes. Spread the Crunch Topping over the pie. Bake for an additional 10 to 15 minutes or until topping is bubbly and golden brown, covering edge of pie crust with foil if needed. Cool.

Yield: 10 servings

CRUNCH TOPPING

$1/3$ cup packed brown sugar
3 tablespoons honey

3 tablespoons butter or margarine
$1^1/2$ cups pecan halves

Combine the brown sugar, honey and butter in a saucepan. Cook over medium heat for 2 to 3 minutes or until the sugar dissolves, stirring constantly. Stir in the pecan halves.

Savannah has been called many things—"the best kept secret in America."
Throughout her over-two centuries, she has continued to cast a spell that has charmed
almost all who have come to know her beautiful squares, her splendid mansions and
plantations, and above all, the unmistakable Savannah cuisine.

Betsy Fancher—Book, *Savannah: A Renaissance of the Heart*

PECAN PIES

2 all ready pie pastries	4 eggs, beaten
1 cup margarine	1 teaspoon lemon juice
1 1/4 cups light corn syrup	2 teaspoons vanilla extract
1 cup sugar	Dash of salt
1 cup packed brown sugar	2 1/2 cups chopped pecans

Prepare the pie pastries using the package directions for two 9-inch baked pie crusts. Cook the margarine in a saucepan until golden brown; cool. Combine the corn syrup, sugar, brown sugar, eggs, lemon juice, vanilla and salt in a bowl and mix well. Stir in the pecans. Add the browned margarine and mix well. Spoon into the prepared pie crusts. Bake at 425 degrees for 10 minutes. Reduce the temperature to 325 degrees. Bake for 40 minutes, covering the edges with foil if needed.

Yield: 6 to 8 servings

BEST PUMPKIN PIE IN GEORGIA

1 1/2 cups mashed cooked pumpkin	1/2 teaspoon ground ginger
1 1/2 cups whipping cream	1/8 teaspoon cloves
1/2 cup packed dark brown sugar	4 eggs, slightly beaten
1/2 teaspoon salt	1 teaspoon vanilla extract
1 teaspoon cinnamon	1 baked (9-inch) pie shell

Combine the pumpkin, whipping cream, brown sugar, salt, cinnamon, ginger, cloves and eggs in the top of a double boiler and mix well. Cook over hot water until mixture thickens, stirring occasionally. Cool slightly. Stir in the vanilla. Pour into the pie shell. Serve with whipped cream.

Yield: 6 to 8 servings

STRAWBERRY CRACKER PIE

3 egg whites	24 butter crackers, crushed
1/2 teaspoon cream of tartar	1 cup whipping cream
1 cup sugar	1/4 cup confectioners' sugar
1 cup chopped pecans	2 cups strawberries, sliced
1 1/2 teaspoons vanilla extract	

Beat the egg whites with the cream of tartar in a mixer bowl until stiff peaks form. Beat in the sugar. Fold in the pecans, 1 teaspoon of the vanilla and the crackers. Spread in a buttered 9- or 10-inch pie plate. Bake at 350 degrees for 30 minutes; cool. Beat the whipping cream in a mixer bowl until foamy. Add the confectioners' sugar gradually, beating until soft peaks form. Fold in the remaining 1/2 teaspoon vanilla and strawberries. Spoon into the cooled cracker crust.

Yield: 6 to 8 servings

BETTER BUTTER FINGERS

1/2 cup butter, softened	1/2 cup chopped nuts
1/3 cup sugar	1 teaspoon vanilla extract
1 1/3 cups self-rising flour	Confectioners' sugar

Combine the butter and sugar in a bowl and mix well. Add the flour, nuts and vanilla and mix by hand. Shape into small rolls. Place on baking sheets. Bake at 250 degrees for 45 minutes. Cool on a wire rack. Roll in confectioners' sugar to coat.

Yield: 1 1/2 dozen cookies

COCONUT MACAROONS

From Savannah Candy Kitchen

2 egg whites $\qquad$ $1/8$ teaspoon salt
$1/2$ teaspoon vanilla extract $\qquad$ 2 tablespoons flour
$1/3$ cup sugar $\qquad$ $1^1/3$ cups shredded coconut

Combine the egg whites, vanilla, sugar, salt and flour in a bowl and mix well. Stir in the coconut. Drop by level teaspoonfuls onto greased cookie sheets. Bake at 350 degrees for 20 minutes.

Yield: 1 $^1/2$ dozen cookies

FORGOTTEN COOKIES

2 egg whites $\qquad$ 1 cup chopped nuts
$3/4$ cup sugar $\qquad$ 1 cup chocolate chips
Pinch of salt

Preheat oven to 350 degrees. Place foil shiny side up on 2 cookie sheets. Beat the egg whites in a mixer bowl until stiff peaks form. Beat in the sugar gradually. Stir in the salt, nuts and chocolate chips. Drop by teaspoonfuls onto prepared cookie sheets. Place in the oven. Turn off the oven and leave cookies for 8 to 12 hours.

Yield: 1 $^1/2$ dozen cookies

Lucy Mouse's Tavern was run by the mother of Peter Tondee's wife, who once got in trouble for selling rum to an Indian woman.
Excerpt from article of *Savannah News* 2/11/99

FRUITCAKE COOKIES

2 cups cake flour	1 pound raisins
1 teaspoon cinnamon	1 pound dates, chopped
1 teaspoon baking soda	1 pound candied cherries
1 cup butter	1 pound candied pineapple
1 cup packed brown sugar	7 cups pecans, chopped
3 eggs, well beaten	

Sift the flour, cinnamon and baking soda together. Cream the butter and brown sugar in a mixer bowl until light and fluffy. Add the eggs and mix well. Add the sifted dry ingredients and mix well. Stir in the raisins, dates, candied cherries, candied pineapple and pecans. Drop by tablespoonfuls onto greased cookie sheets. Bake at 300 degrees for 30 minutes or until brown. Cool on a wire rack.

Yield: 4 dozen cookies

COTTON EXCHANGE MOLASSES CRINKLES

$3/4$ cup shortening	$1/4$ teaspoon salt
1 egg	$1/2$ teaspoon cloves
$1/4$ cup molasses	1 teaspoon cinnamon
1 cup packed brown sugar	1 teaspoon ginger
$2^1/4$ cups flour	Sugar
2 teaspoons baking powder	

Combine the shortening, egg and molasses in a bowl and mix well. Combine the brown sugar, flour, baking powder, salt, cloves, cinnamon and ginger in a bowl and mix well. Add to the molasses mixture and mix well. Chill, covered, until firm. Shape into balls. Dip the tops in a small amount of sugar. Place on nonstick cookie sheets. Bake at 375 degrees for 10 to 12 minutes or until set.

Yield: 2 dozen cookies

BANANA OATMEAL COOKIES

$1^1/_2$ cups flour $^3/_4$ cup shortening

$^1/_2$ teaspoon baking soda 1 cup sugar

$^1/_2$ teaspoon baking powder 1 egg

$^1/_4$ teaspoon salt 1 cup mashed bananas

$^3/_4$ teaspoon cinnamon 1 cup quick-cooking oats

$^1/_4$ teaspoon nutmeg

Combine the flour, baking soda, baking powder, salt, cinnamon and nutmeg in a bowl and mix well. Cream the shortening and sugar in a mixer bowl until light and fluffy. Beat in the egg. Stir in the bananas and oats. Add the dry ingredients and mix well. Drop by teaspoonfuls onto greased cookie sheets. Bake at 400 degrees for 13 minutes. Cool on wire racks.

Yield: 6 dozen cookies

RICHARD'S OATMEAL COOKIES

From Bodi's

$1^1/_2$ cups sifted flour 2 eggs

1 teaspoon salt 1 teaspoon vanilla extract

1 teaspoon baking soda 3 cups rolled oats

1 cup butter 1 cup chopped pecans

1 cup packed brown sugar 1 cup raisins

1 cup sugar

Sift the flour, salt and baking soda together. Cream the butter, brown sugar and sugar in a mixer bowl until light and fluffy. Add the eggs and mix well. Add the sifted dry ingredients and mix well. Add the vanilla and mix well. Stir in the oats, pecans and raisins. May be chilled until firm. Drop by teaspoonfuls onto greased cookie sheets. Bake at 350 degrees for 10 to 15 minutes or until lightly browned. *Tip:* Batter may be frozen in teaspoonfuls and baked as needed.

Yield: 4 dozen cookies

IRRESISTIBLE PEANUT BUTTER COOKIES

1³/4 cups flour
¹/2 cup sugar
¹/2 teaspoon baking soda
¹/4 teaspoon salt
¹/2 cup butter
¹/2 cup creamy peanut butter

¹/4 cup honey
1 tablespoon milk
24 miniature chocolate-coated caramel-topped nougat bars with peanuts

Preheat oven to 350 degrees. Combine the flour, sugar, baking soda and salt in a bowl and mix well. Cut in the butter and peanut butter until crumbly. Beat in honey and milk until well mixed. Shape by tablespoonfuls into 2-inch circles on a lightly floured surface. Place 1 nougat in the center of each circle. Shape the dough around the nougats to form balls. Place on cookie sheets. Bake for 12 to 15 minutes or until edges are lightly browned. Cool on a wire rack. *Tip:* Regular-size candy bars cut into 1-inch squares may be substituted for the miniature candy bars.

Yield: 24 cookies

PECAN BUTTERBALLS

2 cups sifted flour
¹/4 cup sugar
¹/2 teaspoon salt

1 cup butter, softened
2 teaspoons vanilla extract
3 cups chopped nuts

Sift the flour, sugar and salt into a bowl. Add the butter and vanilla and mix well. Stir in 2 cups of the nuts. Shape into 1-inch balls. Roll in the remaining 1 cup of nuts to coat. Place on nonstick cookie sheets. Bake at 325 degrees for 25 minutes. Cool on a wire rack.

Yield: 4¹/2 dozen cookies

Pecan Puffs

3 ounces cream cheese, softened	1 egg
$1/2$ cup margarine, softened	1 teaspoon vanilla extract
1 cup sifted flour	1 tablespoon melted margarine
$2/3$ cup packed brown sugar	1 cup finely chopped pecans

Combine the cream cheese, margarine and flour in a bowl and mix well. Shape into 24 balls. Press over the bottom and up the side of 24 miniature muffin cups. Combine the brown sugar, egg, vanilla and margarine in a bowl and mix well. Stir in the pecans. Spoon evenly into the pastry shells. Bake at 375 degrees for 20 minutes.

Yield: 2 dozen puffs

Best-Ever Refrigerator Cookies

A delicious holiday cookie.

$3^1/2$ cups flour	1 cup butter, softened
$1/2$ teaspoon salt	2 eggs
1 teaspoon baking soda	$1^1/2$ teaspoons vanilla extract
1 (1-pound) package dark brown sugar	1 cup chopped nuts

Sift the flour, salt and baking soda together. Cream the brown sugar and butter in a mixer bowl until light and fluffy. Add the eggs and vanilla and mix well. Add the sifted dry ingredients and mix well. Stir in the nuts. Chill in the refrigerator until cool. Shape into 1x4-inch rolls. Cover with waxed paper. Chill in the refrigerator for 4 to 6 hours or until cold. Cut into thin slices. Place on greased cookie sheets. Bake at 400 degrees for 4 to 6 minutes or until lightly browned. Cool on a wire rack.

Yield: $3^1/2$ dozen cookies

BABE RUTH BARS

6 cups cornflakes
2 cups Spanish peanuts
1¹/2 cups light corn syrup
1 cup packed brown sugar
1 cup sugar

1 cup creamy peanut butter
2 (16-ounce) packages milk chocolate chips or an equal amount of candy bars

Combine the cornflakes and peanuts in a large bowl. Combine the corn syrup, brown sugar and sugar in a saucepan. Cook over medium heat until the brown sugar and sugar are dissolved, stirring frequently. Add the peanut butter, stirring until melted. Pour over the cornflake mixture and mix well. Press over the bottom of an 11x14-inch baking pan. Sprinkle the chocolate chips over the top. Bake at 200 degrees for 8 minutes. Spread the warm chocolate evenly over the top. Cool. Cut into bars.

Yield: 3 dozen bars

BOURBON BROWNIES

1 (23-ounce) package brownie mix
2 eggs
1 cup chopped walnuts
6 tablespoons bourbon

¹/2 cup butter, softened
2 cups confectioners' sugar
3 tablespoons rum
6 ounces semisweet chocolate
¹/4 cup butter

Combine the brownie mix, eggs and walnuts in a bowl and mix well. Bake using the package directions. Sprinkle with the bourbon; cool. Combine ¹/2 cup butter, confectioners' sugar and rum in a bowl and mix well. Spread over the brownies; chill. Combine the chocolate and ¹/4 cup butter in a small saucepan. Heat until butter and chocolate are melted, stirring constantly. Drizzle over the top; chill. Cut into bars.

Yield: 15 brownies

BODACIOUS BROWNIES

1¹/2 cups flour	2 cups sugar
1 teaspoon salt	4 eggs
1 teaspoon baking powder	2 to 3 teaspoons vanilla extract
¹/4 cup (heaping) baking cocoa	1¹/2 cups chopped pecans
1 cup butter	Cocoa Icing

Sift the flour, salt and baking powder together. Combine the baking cocoa and butter in a saucepan. Cook over medium heat until butter is melted, stirring frequently. Pour into a mixer bowl. Add the sugar and mix well. Beat in eggs 1 at a time, mixing well after each addition. Beat in the sifted dry ingredients. Stir in the vanilla and pecans. Spoon into a greased 6x11-inch baking pan; do not use a glass baking dish. Bake at 350 degrees for 25 to 30 minutes or until brownies pull from the sides of the pan. Cool completely. Frost with Cocoa Icing. Cut into bars.

Yield: 2 dozen brownies

COCOA ICING

¹/4 cup baking cocoa	1 tablespoon vanilla extract
¹/2 cup butter	¹/4 cup (about) evaporated milk
1 (1-pound) package confectioners' sugar	

Combine the baking cocoa and butter in a saucepan. Cook over medium heat until butter is melted, stirring frequently. Stir in the confectioners' sugar and vanilla. Add the evaporated milk gradually. Cook until bubbly and glossy, stirring constantly.

For Savannah natives whose ancestors hacked the city out of marshes, underbrush and pine trees, the past years and the accompanying changes have passed quickly. The relaxed country life now is reserved mostly for weekends when people take to the beach or the gay life of the Riverfront clubs or to private gardens on nearby islands where wine and wisteria mix perfectly with Japonica and gin.

Page 127, Excerpt from Edward Chang Sieg, *Eden on the Marsh: An Illustrated History of Savannah, 1985.* Windsor Publications.

Praline Brownies

1/2 cup packed dark brown sugar	2 eggs
3/4 cup margarine or butter	1 1/2 cups flour
2 tablespoons evaporated milk	1 teaspoon vanilla extract
1/2 cup coarsely chopped pecans	1/2 teaspoon salt
2 cups packed light brown sugar	

Combine the dark brown sugar, 1/4 cup of the margarine and evaporated milk in a saucepan. Cook over low heat until margarine is melted, stirring constantly. Pour into an 8x8-inch baking pan. Sprinkle the pecans over the layer. Cream the light brown sugar and remaining 1/2 cup margarine in a mixer bowl until light and fluffy. Add the eggs and mix well. Add the flour, vanilla and salt, stirring just until moistened. Spread over the pecans. Bake at 350 degrees for 45 to 50 minutes or until brownies pull from the sides of the pan. Cool for 5 minutes. Invert onto a tray or serving plate; cool slightly. Cut into squares.

Yield: 16 brownies

Caramel Apple Oat Squares

1 3/4 cups flour	1 cup chopped walnuts
1 cup quick-cooking oats	20 caramel squares
1/2 cup packed brown sugar	1 (14-ounce) can sweetened condensed milk
1/2 teaspoon baking soda	
1/2 teaspoon salt	1 (21-ounce) can apple pie filling or topping
1 cup cold margarine	

Preheat oven to 375 degrees. Combine the flour, oats, brown sugar, baking soda and salt in a bowl and mix well. Cut in the margarine until crumbly. Reserve 1 1/2 cups of the crumb mixture. Press the remaining crumb mixture over the bottom of a 9x13-inch baking pan. Bake for 15 minutes. Stir the walnuts into the reserved crumb mixture. Melt the caramels with the condensed milk in a saucepan over low heat, stirring until smooth. Layer the apple pie filling, caramel mixture and reserved crumb mixture over the baked layer. Bake for 20 minutes or until set; cool. Cut into squares. Serve warm with ice cream.

Yield: 3 dozen squares

CHOCOLATE CREAM CHEESE SQUARES

This recipe is a favorite because you can use different cake mix flavors!
We think chocolate is the best.

$^{1}/_{2}$ cup butter
1 (2-layer) package Swiss chocolate cake mix
1 egg, slightly beaten
1 cup chopped pecans
8 ounces cream cheese, softened
1 (1-pound) package confectioners' sugar
2 eggs
1 teaspoon vanilla extract

Melt the butter in a saucepan. Combine the butter, cake mix and beaten egg in a bowl and mix well. Stir in the pecans. Press over the bottom of a 9x13-inch baking pan. Combine the cream cheese, confectioners' sugar, 2 eggs and vanilla in a mixer bowl. Beat until smooth. Pour over the cake mix mixture. Bake at 325 degrees for 45 minutes. Cool. Cut into squares.

Yield: 30 to 36 squares

The Forsyth Park Fountain was erected in 1858 and is similar in design to the grand fountain in Paris in the Place de la Concorde. It is the most visited attraction by tourists in the city. The fountain is located in Forsyth Park, named for former Georgia governor John Forsyth.

Savannah: People, Places and Events. Ron Freeman, 1998.

Pecan Squares

1 cup butter or margarine
1 cup sugar
1 egg yolk
1 teaspoon vanilla extract
2 cups flour

1 teaspoon baking soda
1 to 2 teaspoons cinnamon
1 egg white
1 cup finely chopped pecans

Cream the butter and sugar in a mixer bowl until light and fluffy. Beat in the egg yolk, vanilla, flour, baking soda and cinnamon; dough will be stiff. Shape into a thin rectangle on a greased baking sheet. Brush with the egg white. Sprinkle pecans over the top. Bake at 325 degrees for 35 minutes. Cut into squares.

Yield: 2 dozen squares

Pumpkin Figaro

16 (about) Fig Newtons
4 ounces cream cheese, softened
$1/2$ cup chunky peanut butter
$1^1/2$ cups puréed pumpkin
1 egg

1 teaspoon pumpkin pie spice
1 tablespoon vanilla extract
5 ounces evaporated milk
Freshly whipped cream

Preheat oven to 350 degrees. Grease and flour an 8x8-inch or 9x9-inch baking pan. Arrange the Fig Newtons over the bottom of the prepared pan, completely covering the bottom. Beat the cream cheese and peanut butter in a mixer bowl until light and fluffy. Spread over the Fig Newtons, sealing to the edges. Combine the pumpkin, egg, pie spice, vanilla and evaporated milk in a bowl and mix well. Pour over the cream cheese layer. Bake for 50 to 60 minutes. Cut into squares.

Yield: 12 squares

FROM
PEANUT BRITTLE
TO
KAHLÚA CAKE

CAKES AND DESSERTS

THE ANDREW LOW HOUSE

MRS. ANDREW LOW'S RECEPTION CAKE

A reception was held at the Andrew Low's elegant residence, on LaFayette Square in Savannah, Georgia, on New Year's Day. Letters in the archives of the Georgia Colonial Dames contain references to these occasions; "yesterday the girls dressed the house with flowers and thirty gentlemen called," was written about New Year's Day 1866. The "girls" were Amy and Hattie, Andrew Low's two elder daughters, whose mother was Sarah Hunter, his first wife.

When William Thackeray was guest at the Lows' twice (1853 and 1856), he wrote of the "excellent table set by my host." Robert E. Lee was a family friend and had courted Mary Low's mother when he was a young lieutenant stationed in Savannah during the construction of Fort Pulaski. A grand reception was held at the Low residence on the occasion of his visit to Savannah in 1870.

Reception Cake

1 lb. Flour (4 cups)

1 lb. Butter (2 cups)

1 1/2 lbs. Sugar (3 cups)

2 Coconuts, grated
    (4-8 oz. packages, frozen)

1 doz. Eggs (12 eggs, separated)

1 1/2 lbs. Blanched Almonds,
    chopped

2 lbs. Citron, chopped
    (reserve one cup flour & mix
    with citron before chopping)

1 Wine Glass Sherry
    (1/2 cup)

1 Wine Glass Brandy
    (1/2 cup)

1/2 tablespoon Nutmeg

1 tablespoon Mace

1 tablespoon Cinnamon

Line two Turks pans (large tube pans) with greased paper (bottom of pan). Prepare a slow oven (275 degrees).

Cream butter and sugar. Beat egg yolks. Add flour and spices to fruit, coconut and nuts. Mix wine into butter and sugar mixture (sherry and brandy). Mix flour, butter and sugar mixtures together. Beat egg whites until stiff, then fold egg whites into flour, etc. mixture.

Divide mixture between two pans and bake at 275 degrees for 3 hours. After 1 hour put a pan of hot water on oven rack beneath cakes. After 3 hours, remove cakes from oven and invert on rack to cool.

This recipe will take about 2 hours to prepare and mix. To serve, slice as you would fruit cake, using a dampened knife and wipe blade after cutting each slice to insure uniform and clean-cut slices. Serve in a silver cake basket or arranged on a silver tray.

GEORGIA PEACH POUND CAKE

3 cups flour
1/4 teaspoon baking soda
1/2 teaspoon salt
1 cup butter, softened
3 cups sugar
6 eggs, at room temperature

1 teaspoon vanilla extract
1/2 teaspoon almond extract
1/2 cup sour cream
2 cups chopped peeled peaches
Cream Cheese Frosting

Preheat oven to 350 degrees. Grease and flour a 10-inch tube pan. Mix the flour, baking soda and salt in a small bowl. Cream the butter and sugar in a mixer bowl until light and fluffy. Add the eggs 1 at a time, mixing well after each addition. Stir in the vanilla and almond extract. Add the dry ingredients and mix well. Fold in the sour cream and peaches. Pour into the prepared pan. Bake for 75 to 85 minutes or until a wooden pick inserted in the center comes out clean. Cool in the pan for 10 minutes. Invert onto a serving plate. Cool completely. Frost with Cream Cheese Frosting.

Yield: 16 servings

CREAM CHEESE FROSTING

8 ounces cream cheese, softened
1/4 cup butter, softened
1 tablespoon milk

1/2 teaspoon almond extract
1 (1-pound) package
confectioners' sugar, sifted

Cream the cream cheese and butter in a mixer bowl until light and fluffy. Add the milk and almond extract and mix well. Add the confectioners' sugar gradually, beating until smooth.

CARAMEL ICING

Brown 1/4 cup sugar in a heavy saucepan. Stir in 1/2 cup water. Cook over low heat until sugar dissolves. Remove from heat. Combine 4 cups sugar and 1 1/2 cups evaporated milk in a large heavy saucepan and mix well. Bring to a boil over medium heat, stirring constantly. Pour in the sugar mixture. Cook, uncovered, over medium heat at 234 to 240 degrees on a candy thermometer, soft-ball stage, stirring frequently. Add 1 cup margarine. Cook until margarine melts, stirring constantly. Remove from heat. Beat by hand until icing is cool enough to spread on a cake. Add additional evaporated milk if needed to make of a spreading consistency.

Yield: 5 cups (Icing for 4 layers)

CARAMEL NUT POUND CAKE

1/2 teaspoon salt

1/2 teaspoon baking powder

3 cups sifted flour

1 cup butter, softened

1/2 cup shortening

1 (1-pound) package brown sugar

1 cup sugar

5 eggs

1 cup milk or cream

1 teaspoon vanilla extract

1 cup walnuts, finely chopped

Preheat oven to 325 degrees. Sift the salt, baking powder and flour together. Cream the butter, shortening and brown sugar in a mixer bowl until light and fluffy. Add the sugar gradually, mixing well. Add the eggs 1 at a time, mixing well after each addition. Add the sifted dry ingredients and milk alternately, mixing well after each addition and beginning and ending with the dry ingredients. Add the vanilla and mix well. Stir in the walnuts. Pour into a greased and floured 10-inch tube pan. Bake for 1 1/2 hours or until a wooden pick inserted in the center comes out clean. Cool in the pan for 15 minutes. Invert onto a serving plate.

Yield: 16 servings

WHIPPED CREAM POUND CAKE

1 cup butter, softened

1 cup whipping cream

3 cups sugar

6 eggs

3 cups cake flour, sifted twice

1 tablespoon vanilla extract

1 teaspoon lemon extract

1 (1-pound) package confectioners' sugar

1/2 cup butter, softened

2 teaspoons vanilla or lemon extract

2 tablespoons (or more) evaporated milk

Combine 1 cup butter, whipping cream, sugar and eggs in a bowl and mix well. Add the flour and mix well. Stir in the vanilla and lemon extract. Pour into a greased 5x9-inch loaf pan. Place in a cold oven. Bake at 250 degrees for 1 1/2 hours. Cool in the pan for 10 minutes. Remove to a wire rack to cool completely. Combine the confectioners' sugar, 1/2 cup butter, vanilla and enough evaporated milk to make of a spreading consistency in a bowl and mix well. Spread over the cooled cake.

Yield: 10 servings

FIVE-FLAVORING POUND CAKE

3 cups flour	1 cup milk
$1/2$ teaspoon salt	1 teaspoon vanilla extract
$1/2$ teaspoon baking powder	1 teaspoon lemon extract
1 cup butter or margarine	1 teaspoon coconut flavoring
$1/2$ cup vegetable shortening	1 teaspoon rum flavoring
3 cups sugar	1 teaspoon butter flavoring
5 eggs, well beaten	Five-Flavoring Glaze (optional)

Preheat oven to 325 degrees. Sift the flour, salt and baking powder together. Cream the butter, shortening and sugar in a mixer bowl until light and fluffy. Add the eggs and mix well. Add the sifted dry ingredients and milk alternately, mixing well after each addition and beginning and ending with the dry ingredients. Stir in the vanilla and lemon extracts and the coconut, rum and butter flavorings. Pour into a greased and floured 10-inch tube pan. Bake for 1 to $1^1/2$ hours or until a wooded pick inserted in the center comes out clean. Pour the Five-Flavoring Glaze over the cake. Cool in the pan for 10 minutes. Invert onto a serving plate. Cool completely.

Yield: 10 servings

FIVE-FLAVORING GLAZE

1 cup sugar	1 teaspoon coconut flavoring
$1/2$ cup water	1 teaspoon rum flavoring
1 teaspoon vanilla extract	1 teaspoon butter flavoring
1 teaspoon lemon extract	

Combine the sugar, water, vanilla and lemon extracts and the coconut, rum and butter flavorings in a saucepan. Bring to a boil. Boil until the sugar dissolves.

Kahlúa Cake

1 cup chopped pecans or walnuts
1 (2-layer) package yellow butter-recipe and pudding-recipe cake mix
1 (3-ounce) package vanilla instant pudding mix
4 eggs
$1/2$ cup cold water
$1/2$ cup vegetable oil
$1/2$ cup Kahlúa or Kamara decaffeinated liqueur
Kahlúa Topping (optional) or a caramel icing

Preheat oven to 350 degrees. Oil and flour a 10-inch tube pan. Sprinkle the pecans over the bottom of the prepared pan; pecans may be mixed into the batter if preferred. Combine the cake mix, pudding mix, eggs, cold water, oil and Kahlúa in a mixer bowl. Beat for 4 minutes or until smooth and creamy. Pour into the prepared pan. Bake for $1^1/4$ to $1^1/2$ hours or until a wooden pick inserted in the center comes out clean. Poke holes in the top of the hot cake. Pour Kahlúa Topping over the cake.

Yield: 10 servings

Kahlúa Topping

$1/2$ cup butter
$1/2$ cup sugar
$1/4$ cup water
$1/4$ cup Kahlúa

Combine the butter, sugar, water and Kahlúa in a saucepan. Bring to a boil. Boil for 3 minutes or until mixture thickens.

Kahlúa

4 cups sugar
3 cups water
$1/2$ cup instant coffee
1 cup boiling water
1 vanilla bean
1 quart vodka

Combine the sugar and water in a saucepan. Bring to a boil. Boil for 20 minutes; cool. Dissolve the coffee in the boiling water; cool. Split the vanilla bean lengthwise. Place in a $1/2$-gallon container. Pour the vodka over the bean. Pour in the sugar mixture. Pour in the coffee. Store, covered, for 2 weeks or longer.

Pecan Pie Cake

From Savannah Candy Kitchen

3 cups finely chopped pecans, toasted
2 cups flour
1 teaspoon baking soda
1/2 cup butter or margarine, softened
1/2 cup shortening

2 cups sugar
5 egg yolks
1 tablespoon vanilla extract
1 cup buttermilk
5 egg whites
3/4 cup dark corn syrup
Pecan Pie Filling

Sprinkle 2 cups of the chopped pecans evenly over the bottoms of 3 buttered 9-inch round cake pans, shaking to coat the bottoms and sides of the pans. Combine the flour and baking soda in a bowl and mix well. Beat the butter and shortening in a mixer bowl at medium speed until light and fluffy. Beat in the sugar gradually. Add the egg yolks 1 at a time, mixing well after each addition. Stir in the vanilla. Add the flour mixture and buttermilk alternately, mixing well after each addition and beginning and ending with the flour mixture. Stir in the remaining 1 cup pecans. Beat the egg whites in a mixer bowl at medium speed until stiff peaks form. Fold 1/3 of the beaten egg whites into the batter. Fold in the remaining egg whites. Pour the batter into the prepared pans. Bake at 350 degrees for 25 minutes or until a wooden pick inserted in the center comes out clean. Cool in the pans on wire racks for 10 minutes. Invert onto waxed-paper-lined wire racks. Brush the tops and sides of the layers with corn syrup. Cool completely. Place 1 layer pecan side up on a serving plate. Spread with half the Pecan Pie Filling. Place the second layer pecan side up on the filling. Spread with the remaining Pecan Pie Filling. Place the third layer pecan side up on the filling.

Yield: 12 to 16 servings

Pecan Pie Filling

1/2 cup packed dark brown sugar
3/4 cup dark corn syrup
1/3 cup cornstarch
4 egg yolks

1 1/2 cups half-and-half
1/8 teaspoon salt
3 tablespoons butter or margarine
1 teaspoon vanilla extract

Whisk the brown sugar, corn syrup, cornstarch, egg yolks, half-and-half and salt in a heavy 3-quart saucepan until smooth. Bring to a boil over medium heat, whisking constantly. Boil for 1 minute or until mixture thickens. Remove from heat. Whisk in the butter and vanilla. Place a sheet of waxed paper on the surface of the mixture. Chill for 4 hours.

MADISON SQUARE STRAWBERRY CAKE

1 (2-layer) package yellow cake mix
3 tablespoons flour
1 cup vegetable oil
1 (3-ounce) package strawberry gelatin
4 eggs

1/2 cup water
1 (10-ounce) package frozen strawberries, thawed
1/2 cup vegetable shortening
1 (1-pound) package confectioners' sugar

Line two 9-inch cake pans with waxed paper. Combine the cake mix, flour, oil and gelatin in a mixer bowl and beat for 2 minutes or until smooth. Add the eggs. Beat for 2 minutes longer or until smooth. Add the water and half the strawberries with juice and mix well. Pour into the prepared pans. Bake at 350 degrees for 30 to 35 minutes or until a wooden pick inserted in the center comes out clean. Cool in the pans for 10 minutes. Remove to a wire rack to cool completely. Combine the shortening and confectioners' sugar in a bowl and mix well. Stir in the remaining strawberries. Spread between the layers and over the top and side of the cooled cake.

Yield: 10 servings

Thanksgiving Day at Fort Pulaski

Seized by Georgia Confederate troops in 1861, the fort was retaken by Federal troops April 11, 1862 with the aid of a new weapon, the rifled cannon. In November of that same year, Fort Pulaski was the scene of a Thanksgiving celebration (though President Abraham Lincoln would not make Thanksgiving a national holiday until 1863).

All of the Federal "Officers and ladies of Beaufort" (Savannah being still in Confederate hands) were invited to attend the "fete" which took place November 27. The visitors embarked upon a boat in Hilton Head for the three hour trip to the fort. One young woman wrote her sister that the fort's cannon fired a salute in their honor, and that "Many Officers were at the landing to receive us and a good many soldiers—all saluted as we passed—A full brass band played . . ." The day was eventful, beginning with a shooting contest followed by rowboat, foot, "Hurdle" sack, and wheelbarrow races, all with purses of ten dollars going to the winners. The races were followed by a "Meal Feat" where competitors, with their hands tied behind their backs, were allowed five minutes to try and seize a five dollar gold piece which had been dropped in a tub of meal with their teeth. Next came greased pole climbing and greased pig catching contests, followed by a Burlesque Dress parade, with the soldiers clad in outlandish outfits.

. . . Archives. Fort Pulaski National Monument. National Park Service.

U.S. Department of the Interior. Savannah, Georgia.

SLO' DEATH BY CHOCOLATE

1 (2-layer) package devil's food
cake mix
1 cup sugar
1/2 cup brewed coffee

3 (9-ounce) packages milk
chocolate mousse mix
3 cups milk
6 Heath bars, crushed

Prepare and bake the cake mix using the package directions for a 9x13-inch cake pan. Combine the sugar and coffee in a saucepan 15 minutes before cake is done. Cook over medium heat for 10 to 15 minutes or until bubbly. Poke holes in the hot cake. Pour the hot coffee mixture over the cake; cool. Crumble the cake. Combine the mousse mix and milk in a saucepan. Cook for 5 to 7 minutes or until thickened, stirring constantly. Remove from heat. Layer the crumbled cake, mousse and crushed Heath bars 1/2 at a time in a clear round bowl. Refrigerate, covered, for 4 days. Serve with whipped cream.

Yield: 20 servings

WHITE FRUITCAKE

2 pounds chopped fruit
1 (8-ounce) package dates
1 pound chopped pecans
1 pound chopped walnuts
1/2 (15-ounce) package white
seedless raisins
3 cups sifted flour
2 1/2 teaspoons baking powder

1 teaspoon salt
1/2 cup orange juice or other
juice
2 tablespoons rum extract
1 cup shortening
1 cup sugar
5 eggs

Grease a 10-inch tube pan. Line with waxed paper. Combine the fruit, dates, pecans, walnuts, raisins and 1 cup of the sifted flour in a large bowl and toss to coat completely with the flour. Combine the remaining 2 cups sifted flour, baking powder and salt in a bowl and mix well. Combine the orange juice and rum extract in a bowl and mix well. Cream the shortening and sugar in a mixer bowl until light and fluffy. Add the eggs 1 at a time, mixing well after each addition. Add the dry ingredients and juice mixture alternately, mixing well after each addition and ending with the dry ingredients. Pour over the fruit mixture and mix gently. Spoon into the prepared pan. Bake at 300 degrees for 2 1/2 hours. Let stand in the pan until completely cooled. Loosen the cake from the side of the pan. Place on a serving plate.

Yield: 16 servings

Wormsloe Éclair Cake

Regular éclairs are very difficult and time-consuming to make. This cake tastes exactly like bakery-quality éclairs without all the fuss!

2 cups water
1 cup margarine
2 cups flour, sifted
8 eggs
2¹/2 cups milk

2 (3-ounce) packages vanilla instant pudding mix
6 ounces nondairy whipped topping
Chocolate Frosting

Combine the water and margarine in a saucepan. Bring to a boil. Remove from heat. Add the flour and mix well. Add the eggs 1 at a time, mixing well after each addition. Shape the dough into a 12-inch ring on a baking sheet. Bake at 400 degrees for 45 to 50 minutes. Remove to a wire rack to cool completely. Beat the milk and pudding mix in a mixer bowl at low speed for 2 minutes. Fold in the whipped topping. Cut the cake into halves. Place the bottom half on a serving plate. Spread the pudding mixture over the bottom half. Place the top half over the pudding mixture. Drizzle with Chocolate Frosting. Store in the refrigerator.

Yield: 16 servings

Chocolate Frosting

1 cup confectioners' sugar
¹/4 cup butter
1 (1-ounce) square unsweetened chocolate

¹/3 cup milk
Pinch of salt
1 teaspoon vanilla extract

Combine the confectioners' sugar, butter, chocolate, milk and salt in a saucepan. Bring to a boil over low heat. Boil for 5 to 8 minutes or until thick. Stir in the vanilla.

In Savannah's early years, the arrival of a single ship might provoke a day long celebration. There was even rejoicing when a privateer carrying smuggled goods coursed up the inland waterway, particularly if there was rum aboard.

Page 39, Excerpt from Edward Chang Sieg, *Eden on the Marsh: An Illustrated History of Savannah*, 1985. Windsor Publications.

CHARLOTTE RUSSE

Ladyfingers   2 envelopes unflavored gelatin
2 cups heavy cream $1/4$ cup cold water
$1/2$ cup sugar   3 tablespoons sherry

Line the bottom and side of a springform pan with ladyfingers. Beat the cream and sugar in a mixer bowl until soft peaks form. Soften the gelatin in the cold water in a microwave-safe bowl. Microwave for 1 minute or until the gelatin dissolves. Stir the gelatin and sherry into the cream mixture. Pour into the prepared pan. Chill until set. Loosen the side of the pan and place on a serving plate.

Yield: 10 servings

LADYFINGERS

4 ounces confectioners' sugar   4 ounces flour
5 egg yolks   5 egg whites, well beaten

Preheat oven to 350 degrees. Line a baking pan with greased parchment paper. Beat the confectioners' sugar and egg yolks in a mixer bowl until pale yellow. Beat in the flour. Fold in the beaten egg whites. Drop the batter by spoonfuls 1 inch apart onto the prepared pan in the desired shape. Bake until lightly browned.

BLACK-TIE CHOCOLATE MARBLED CHEESECAKE

1 cup graham cracker crumbs
1/4 cup baking cocoa
3 tablespoons sugar
1/4 cup butter, melted
24 ounces cream cheese, softened
1 cup sugar

2 teaspoons vanilla extract
3 eggs
4 (1-ounce) squares semisweet chocolate
Chocolate Glaze

Combine the graham cracker crumbs, baking cocoa and sugar in a bowl and mix well. Add the butter and mix well. Press over the bottom of a 9-inch springform pan. Chill until firm. Preheat oven to 300 degrees. Cream the cream cheese, sugar and vanilla in a mixer bowl until light and fluffy. Add the eggs 1 at a time, mixing well after each addition. Heat the chocolate in a small saucepan until melted, stirring constantly. Combine the melted chocolate and half the cream cheese mixture in a bowl and mix well. Pour half the remaining cream cheese mixture over the crust, spreading evenly. Pour half the chocolate cream cheese mixture over the layer, spreading evenly. Pour the remaining cream cheese mixture over the chocolate layer, spreading evenly. Drizzle the remaining chocolate cream cheese mixture over the top. Draw a knife through the batter to marbleize. Bake for 1 hour. Turn off the oven. Let the cheesecake stand in the warm oven for 1 hour. Remove from oven. Loosen from the side of the pan. Cool completely. Remove the side of the pan. Spread Chocolate Glaze over the top and side of the cheesecake. Store in the refrigerator.

Yield: 10 servings

CHOCOLATE GLAZE

4 (1-ounce) squares semisweet chocolate

1/4 cup butter

Melt the chocolate and butter in a small saucepan over low heat, stirring constantly.

Dot's Sweet Potato Pecan Cheesecake

1 (6-ounce) package zwieback crackers, crushed

1/4 cup sugar

6 tablespoons butter, melted

24 ounces cream cheese, softened

3/4 cup sugar

1 3/4 cups packed brown sugar

5 eggs

2 cups mashed cooked sweet potatoes

1 teaspoon cinnamon

1/2 teaspoon nutmeg

1/2 teaspoon ground ginger

1/4 cup whipping cream

6 tablespoons butter, softened

1 cup pecans, coarsely chopped

Combine the crackers, sugar and melted butter in a bowl and mix well. Press over the bottom and up the side of a greased 9-inch springform pan; chill. Beat the cream cheese in a mixer bowl at medium speed until light and fluffy. Beat in the sugar and 3/4 cup of the brown sugar gradually. Beat in the eggs 1 at a time, mixing well after each addition. Beat in the sweet potatoes, cinnamon, nutmeg and ginger. Beat in the cream at low speed. Pour into the prepared crust. Bake at 325 degrees for 1 hour and 35 minutes. Combine the softened butter, remaining 1 cup brown sugar and pecans in a bowl and mix until crumbly. Sprinkle over the cheesecake. Bake for an additional 10 minutes. Cool on a wire rack. Refrigerate, covered, for 4 hours or longer. Remove the side of the pan and place on a serving plate. Garnish with whipped cream and pecans.

Yield: 10 servings

The entertainments of the Soiree Club and German Club were the highlights of the season—later these two clubs combining to form the present Cotillion Club. But they were more generous with their parties in those days, for each club gave six or eight dances. This from a December, 1891 issue, shows who were running the Soiree Club then:
The Soiree Club has its fourth soiree at the DeSoto next Thursday. This is the most beautiful event of the season, in the estimation of those fortunate enough to be present.
. . . One of the most interesting features of the German [club] was the first appearance of five attractive debutantes, Miss Backus, Miss Hayward, Miss Habersham, Miss Guerard and Miss McAlpin. . . . Mr T. M. Cummingham, Jr. will lead the German to be given on December 15.
Savannah Evening Press: "Society of Gay '90's [1891] as Chronicled by the Press"
by Katharine Charlton, Society Editor.

Two-Version Praline Cheesecake

From Bodi's

1 cup graham cracker crumbs
1/4 cup finely chopped pecans
1/4 cup butter, melted
24 ounces cream cheese, softened

1 1/4 cups packed brown sugar
3 eggs
2 teaspoons vanilla extract
1 cup whipping cream

Combine the graham cracker crumbs, pecans and butter in a bowl and mix well. Press over the bottom of a 9-inch springform pan; chill. Beat the cream cheese in a mixer bowl until light and fluffy. Beat in 1 cup of the brown sugar gradually. Beat in the eggs 1 at a time, mixing well after each addition. Beat in the vanilla. Stir in the whipping cream. Pour into the prepared crust. Sprinkle with the remaining 1/4 cup brown sugar. Bake at 450 degrees for 10 minutes. Reduce the oven temperature to 275 degrees. Bake for 1 hour. Cool on a wire rack. Remove the side of the pan and place on a serving plate.

Yield: 10 servings

Colonial Apple Pear Cobbler

1 (20-ounce) can apple pie filling
1 (16-ounce) can sliced pears, drained
1/3 cup dried cranberries
2/3 cup orange juice
2 teaspoons cornstarch
3/4 teaspoon nutmeg

1 1/2 cups reduced-fat buttermilk baking mix
2/3 cup 2% milk
2 tablespoons sugar
2 tablespoons butter or margarine, melted
2 teaspoons sugar

Combine the pie filling, pears and cranberries in an 8x8-inch baking dish and mix well. Combine the orange juice, cornstarch and 1/2 teaspoon of the nutmeg in a bowl and mix well. Stir into the pie filling mixture. Combine the baking mix, milk, 2 tablespoons sugar and butter in a bowl. Stir just until moistened. Drop 6 equal spoonfuls over the pie filling mixture. Combine 2 teaspoons sugar and the remaining 1/4 teaspoon nutmeg in a bowl and mix well. Sprinkle over the top. Bake at 400 degrees for 45 minutes or until fruit is bubbly and topping is cooked through, covering with foil to prevent burning if needed. Serve with vanilla ice cream or frozen yogurt.

Yield: 9 servings

GRANDMA'S PEACH COBBLER

$^{1}/_{2}$ cup butter   1 tablespoon baking powder
1 cup sugar $^{1}/_{2}$ teaspoon salt
1 cup milk   1 teaspoon flavoring of choice
1 cup flour   2 cups chopped peaches

Cream the butter and sugar in a bowl until light and fluffy. Add the milk, flour and baking powder gradually and mix well. Stir in the salt. Add the flavoring and beat until combined. Place the peaches in a buttered 8- or 9-inch square baking dish. Pour the batter over the peaches and stir to combine. Bake at 400 degrees for 45 to 60 minutes.

Yield: 9 servings

PUMPKIN CARAMEL CUSTARD

$1^{1}/_{2}$ cups sugar $1^{1}/_{2}$ teaspoons cinnamon
$^{1}/_{2}$ cup water $^{1}/_{2}$ teaspoon nutmeg
$^{1}/_{2}$ cup puréed cooked pumpkin $^{1}/_{4}$ teaspoon ground ginger
4 eggs, lightly beaten   2 cups low-fat milk, scalded
2 tablespoons vanilla extract

Combine 1 cup of the sugar and water in a heavy saucepan. Cook over medium heat until the sugar dissolves, washing down the sides with a brush dipped in water. Cook over medium heat for 15 minutes or until a deep caramel color, gently swirling the pan occasionally; do not stir. Divide the caramel among six $^{3}/_{4}$-cup ramekins, swirling to coat the bottoms and sides; cool. Preheat oven to 350 degrees. Combine the pumpkin, remaining $^{1}/_{2}$ cup sugar, eggs, vanilla, cinnamon, nutmeg and ginger in a bowl and mix well. Whisk in the scalded milk. Divide among the prepared ramekins. Place the ramekins in a baking dish. Cover the tops with foil. Pour hot water into the dish to reach halfway up the outsides of the ramekins. Bake for 45 to 50 minutes or until set. Remove from the baking dish. Cool on a wire rack. Loosen from the sides. Invert onto serving plates. *Tip:* May be made up to 2 days in advance and stored, covered, in the refrigerator. Place ramekins in a tray with $^{1}/_{2}$ inch hot water and let stand for 5 minutes before inverting.

Yield: 6 servings

ICE CREAM CRUNCH

Vanilla wafers   1 (7-ounce) chocolate crunch
1 gallon vanilla ice cream,   candy bar, frozen
softened   Chocolate Sauce (below)

Arrange vanilla wafers in a layer over the bottom of a pan. Spread half the ice cream over the wafers. Shave the candy bar. Sprinkle over the ice cream. Cover with the remaining ice cream. Freeze until firm. Cut into squares. Drizzle with Chocolate Sauce.

Yield: Variable

HOT FUDGE SAUCE

With a sauce this wonderful, it's easy to get impatient while cooking. But don't try to rush it; keeping the heat low eliminates the danger of scorching the chocolate.

$^1/_2$ cup baking cocoa   3 tablespoons margarine or
$^1/_3$ cup sugar   butter
$^1/_3$ cup packed dark brown sugar $^1/_2$ cup whipping cream

Combine the baking cocoa, sugar and brown sugar in a bowl and mix well. Combine the margarine and cream in a heavy saucepan. Cook over low heat until the margarine is melted, stirring constantly. Cook over medium heat for 3 minutes or until mixture bubbles around the edges, stirring constantly. Stir in the cocoa mixture. Cook for 1 to 2 minutes or until sugar is dissolved and mixture is smooth and thickened, stirring constantly. Serve immediately or store, covered, in the refrigerator for up to 1 week. To reheat on stovetop, place sauce in a heavy saucepan and cook over low heat, stirring frequently. To reheat in the microwave, place sauce in a 2-cup measure and microwave on High for 1 to 2 minutes or until heated through.

Yield: 4 ($^1/_4$-cup) servings

CHOCOLATE SAUCE

Combine 1 cup sugar, 1 cup evaporated milk, $^1/_4$ cup butter and $^1/_4$ cup light corn syrup in a saucepan. Bring to a boil. Boil for 3 minutes. Add 1 chopped 7-ounce milk chocolate bar. Cook over low heat until the chocolate is melted, stirring constantly.

175

THREE-GENERATIONS BREAD PUDDING

This is an old family recipe and a true pudding. It always gets raves.

Butter	Pinch of salt
3 or 4 slices raisin bread	1 teaspoon vanilla extract
2 cups milk	1 teaspoon nutmeg
$^3/_4$ cup sugar	Brandy Sauce
3 eggs, beaten	

Spread butter over the bread slices. Toast and cool. Tear the toast into small pieces. Place in a 9x13-inch baking pan. Combine 1 cup of the milk and the sugar in a saucepan. Heat until sugar dissolves, stirring frequently. Remove from heat. Combine the remaining cup of milk, eggs, salt and vanilla in a bowl and mix well. Add the sugar mixture and mix well. Pour over the toast. Sprinkle with nutmeg. Bake at 325 degrees for 30 to 35 minutes or until a knife inserted in the center comes out clean. Serve with Brandy Sauce.

Yield: 15 servings

BRANDY SAUCE

1 egg	Pinch of salt
$^1/_3$ cup butter, melted	2 to 3 tablespoons brandy
1 cup sifted confectioners' sugar	1 cup whipping cream

Beat the egg in a mixer bowl until light and fluffy. Beat in the butter, confectioners' sugar, salt and brandy. Beat the cream in a separate mixer bowl until stiff peaks form. Fold into the brandy mixture. Chill, covered, until ready to serve; stir.

BLUEBERRY SAUCE

Combine 2 teaspoons cornstarch and 1 tablespoon water in a saucepan and mix well.
Stir in $^1/_4$ cup sugar, $^1/_3$ cup water or blueberry syrup and $^1/_8$ teaspoon salt. Cook until clear and thickened, stirring constantly. Stir in 2 cups washed, drained blueberries.
Bring to a boil. Boil for 2 to 3 minutes. Serve warm or cold.
Yield: 8 ($^1/_4$-cup) servings

DATE PUDDING

1 cup flour	$1^1/4$ cups boiling water
$1^1/2$ cups packed brown sugar	1 cup chopped pecans or walnuts
1 teaspoon baking powder	1 tablespoon margarine or butter
$^1/2$ cup milk	1 teaspoon vanilla extract
1 cup chopped pitted dates	

Combine the flour, $^3/4$ cup of the brown sugar and baking powder and mix well. Add the milk and mix well. Stir in the dates. Spread over the bottom of a greased 2-quart rectangular baking dish. Combine the boiling water, pecans, remaining $^3/4$ cup brown sugar, margarine and vanilla and mix well. Pour over the date mixture. Bake at 350 degrees for 30 minutes or until set. Serve warm with unsweetened whipped cream.

Yield: 12 to 16 servings

BROWN RICE PUDDING

3 eggs	$1^1/3$ cups brown rice, cooked
$^1/3$ cup honey or maple syrup	$^1/2$ cup raisins
3 cups milk	$^1/2$ cup unsweetened shredded coconut
1 teaspoon vanilla extract	$^1/2$ cup finely chopped almonds
$^1/2$ teaspoon cinnamon	1 cup unsweetened crushed pineapple, drained (optional)
$^1/4$ teaspoon nutmeg	$^1/2$ cup wheat germ (optional)
$^1/4$ teaspoon cloves	

Beat the eggs with the honey in a large bowl until smooth. Add the milk, vanilla, cinnamon, nutmeg and cloves and mix well. Stir in the rice, raisins, coconut, almonds, pineapple and wheat germ. Spoon into a greased $2^1/2$-quart baking dish. Set the dish in a baking pan. Fill the pan 1 inch deep with hot water. Bake at 350 degrees for 45 to 60 minutes or until a knife inserted in the center comes out clean.

Yield: 12 to 16 servings

TIPSY TRIFLE PUDDING

A traditional Thanksgiving and Christmas dinner dessert, the pudding is similar to
Carolina Trifle but has a little more kick. Prepare a bowl without the bourbon for the children.
Graduating to the grownup bowl is a rite of passage.

3 cups milk

9 egg yolks

1 cup sugar

1^1/$_2$ teaspoons vanilla extract

^{1}/$_2$ cup flour

2 packages ladyfingers or angel food cake, cut into strips

1 (12-ounce) jar strawberry preserves

1 cup (about) bourbon or spiced rum

2 cups whipping cream

1 teaspoon sugar

Bring the milk to a boil in a saucepan. Set aside. Combine the egg yolks, 1 cup sugar and vanilla in a bowl. Whisk for 4 minutes or until the mixture forms a ribbon. Whisk in the flour. Pour in half the warm milk and mix well. Pour into the saucepan with the remaining milk. Bring to a boil over medium heat, stirring constantly. Reduce the heat. Cook for 2 to 3 minutes or until smooth and thick, stirring constantly. Chill in the refrigerator until completely cooled. Separate and split the ladyfingers. Spread one of each ladyfinger half with the strawberry preserves and dip the other half in the bourbon. Line the bottom and side of a 3- to 4-quart bowl with the ladyfingers, alternating strawberry and bourbon fingers. Spoon ^{1}/$_3$ of the custard into the bowl, adding milk if needed to thin the custard. May sprinkle a few drops of bourbon over the custard if desired. Arrange a layer of ladyfingers over the custard, alternating strawberry and bourbon fingers. Repeat with a layer of custard, a layer of ladyfingers and a layer of custard. Chill, covered, in the refrigerator. Whip the cream in a mixer bowl with 1 teaspoon sugar until stiff peaks form. Spread over the top of the custard. Garnish with fresh strawberry slices.

Yield: 8 to 10 servings

COLD LIME SOUFFLÉ

1 envelope unflavored gelatin	$1^1/4$ cups sugar
$^1/4$ cup cold water	5 egg whites
5 egg yolks	1 cup whipping cream
$^3/4$ cup lime juice	Lime Sauce
1 tablespoon grated lime peel	

Soften the gelatin in the cold water in a bowl. Combine the egg yolks, lime juice, lime peel and sugar in a saucepan and mix well. Cook over low heat for 8 minutes or until mixture begins to thicken, stirring constantly. Remove from heat. Add the softened gelatin and stir until completely dissolved. Chill for 20 minutes. Beat the egg whites in a mixer bowl until stiff peaks form. Fold into the lime mixture. Whip the cream until stiff peaks form. Fold into the lime mixture. Pour into a 2-quart soufflé dish. Chill for 4 hours or longer. Serve with Lime Sauce.

Yield: 6 to 8 servings

LIME SAUCE

$^1/2$ cup sugar	2 teaspoons grated lime peel
1 tablespoon cornstarch	2 tablespoons butter
$^1/2$ cup water	$^1/4$ cup dry white wine
3 tablespoons lime juice	(optional)

Combine the sugar and cornstarch in a saucepan and mix well. Add the water, lime juice and lime peel and mix well. Add the butter. Bring to a boil, stirring constantly. Reduce the heat. Cook until mixture thickens, stirring constantly. Remove from heat. Stir in the wine. Chill, in the refrigerator. Bring to room temperature before using.

MOTHER'S LEMON SAUCE

Combine 1 cup sugar, 2 tablespoons (scant) flour, salt to taste, $^1/2$ cup hot water, $^1/4$ cup lemon juice and a dash of nutmeg in a bowl and mix well.

LEMON MERINGUE TORTE

3 egg whites	4 egg yolks
$1^1/_2$ cups sugar	$1/_4$ cup lemon juice
$1/_8$ teaspoon cream of tartar	2 tablespoons grated lemon peel
$1/_8$ teaspoon salt	2 cups whipping cream
$3/_4$ teaspoon lemon juice or vinegar	

Beat the egg whites in a mixer bowl until stiff peaks form. Beat in $1/_2$ cup of the sugar gradually. Beat in the cream of tartar and salt. Beat in the $3/_4$ teaspoon lemon juice and $1/_2$ cup of the sugar alternately, mixing well after each addition. Beat until stiff and glossy. Spread in a greased 9-inch round baking pan. Bake at 275 degrees for 40 minutes. Cool in the oven. Beat the egg yolks in a mixer bowl until thick and pale yellow. Beat in the remaining $1/_2$ cup sugar gradually. Stir in the lemon juice and peel. Pour into the top of a double boiler. Cook over hot water for 5 to 8 minutes or until thick, stirring constantly. Remove from heat and cool. Beat the whipping cream in a mixer bowl until stiff peaks form. Spread half the whipped cream over the cooled meringue shell. Spread the lemon mixture over the whipped cream. Spread the remaining whipped cream over the lemon mixture. Chill, covered, for 12 hours or longer.

Yield: 6 servings

STRAWBERRY MERINGUE TORTE

6 egg whites, at room temperature	$1/_4$ teaspoon salt
2 teaspoons vinegar	2 cups sugar
2 teaspoons vanilla extract	Nondairy whipped topping
1 teaspoon almond extract	Sliced strawberries

Line the bottoms of two 9-inch round baking pans with unglazed paper. Beat the egg whites until frothy. Add the vinegar, vanilla, almond extract and salt and beat slightly. Add the sugar gradually, beating well after each addition. Beat until stiff peaks form. Spread evenly over the bottoms of the prepared pans. Bake at 300 degrees for 35 to 40 minutes. Turn off the oven and open the door 1 to 2 inches. Let torte layers stand for 30 minutes. Remove to wire racks to cool completely. Remove from pans. Place one layer on a serving plate. Spread with half the whipped topping. Arrange sliced strawberries over the whipped topping. Repeat with the remaining layer, whipped topping and sliced strawberries. Place a dollop of whipped topping in the center over the strawberries.

Yield: 6 to 8 servings

PEANUT BUTTER BALLS

2 cups margarine,
softened
1 (16-ounce) jar peanut butter
2 (1-pound) packages
confectioners' sugar

3 cups semisweet chocolate chips
or 78 silver bells
1 or 2 ($1^1/2$-ounce) chocolate
bars
$1/2$ to 1 (4-ounce) bar paraffin

Combine the margarine, peanut butter and confectioners' sugar in a bowl and mix well. Shape into small balls. Place on waxed paper in the refrigerator. Melt the chocolate chips, chocolate bars and paraffin in the top of a double boiler, stirring constantly. Dip the balls in the chocolate mixture to coat, using a wooden pick. Place on waxed paper to harden.

Yield: 8 to 12 dozen balls

CARAMEL BALLS

1 (14-ounce) can sweetened
condensed milk
3 ounces cream cheese, softened

Chopped nuts
Whipped cream

Pour the condensed milk into a shallow baking dish and cover with foil. Place the baking dish in a larger pan of hot water. Bake at 425 degrees for 1 hour or until thick and caramel colored. Cool. Refrigerate for 8 to 12 hours. Shape into 24 portions, flattening into circles. Cut the cream cheese into small pieces. Shape each piece into a small ball. Place 1 ball in the center of each slice. Fold the circle in half over the cream cheese. Fold the ends over and shape into a ball. Refrigerate, covered, for up to 3 weeks. Roll the balls in chopped nuts 1 hour before serving. Place 3 balls on each dessert plate. Top with a large dollop of whipped cream. May be served singly as candy.

Yield: 8 servings

STRAWBERRY SAUCE

Bring 1 cup water to a boil in a large saucepan. Add 1 small package sugar-free strawberry gelatin, stirring until dissolved. Stir in one 16-ounce package thawed frozen whole strawberries (cut into halves). Cook over medium-high heat for 5 minutes, stirring occasionally. Mix $1/2$ cup water and 3 tablespoons cornstarch in a bowl. Pour into the strawberry mixture. Bring to a boil. Boil for 1 minute, stirring constantly. Remove from heat. Serve warm.

Peanut Brittle

From Savannah Candy Kitchen

2 cups sugar
1 cup light corn syrup
$^1/_2$ cup water
2 cups peanuts

1 teaspoon (rounded) butter
1 teaspoon vanilla extract
2 teaspoons (heaping) baking soda

Combine the sugar, corn syrup and water in a saucepan and mix well. Cook until a hard ball forms in cold water. Stir in the peanuts and butter. Cook until the syrup begins to brown. Stir in the vanilla. Remove from heat. Add the baking soda and mix well. Pour into a thin layer in buttered pans. Cool until firm. Break into pieces.

Yield: 8 to 10 servings

Georgia Peanut Butter Chocolate Fudge

2 cups peanut butter chips
1 (14-ounce) can sweetened condensed milk

$^1/_4$ cup butter or margarine
1 cup semisweet chocolate chips

Line an 8x8-inch baking pan with waxed paper. Combine the peanut butter chips, 1 cup of the condensed milk and 2 tablespoons of the butter in a heavy saucepan. Cook over low heat until the butter and peanut butter chips are melted, stirring occasionally. Pour into the prepared pan. Combine the chocolate chips, remaining condensed milk and remaining 2 tablespoons butter in a heavy saucepan. Cook over low heat until the butter and chocolate chips are melted. Spread over the peanut butter layer. Chill in the refrigerator for 2 hours. Remove from pan. Cut into squares. Store at room temperature.

Yield: 5 dozen

BUTTERSCOTCH DIP FOR APPLES

Combine two 12-ounce packages butterscotch chips, 2 cans sweetened condensed milk,
1 tablespoon cinnamon and 2 tablespoons white vinegar in a heavy saucepan.
Cook until smooth and well blended, stirring constantly.

WHITE FUDGE

3 cups sugar	2 tablespoons butter
1 cup sour cream	2 teaspoons vanilla extract
1/3 cup light corn syrup	1 1/2 cups chopped nuts
1/4 teaspoon salt	

Combine the sugar, sour cream, corn syrup, salt and butter in a saucepan. Cook over medium heat until the sugar is dissolved and the mixture boils. Reduce the heat. Cook, covered, for 5 minutes. Remove the cover. Boil over high heat until the mixture reaches 234 to 240 degrees on a candy thermometer. Stir in the vanilla and nuts. Pour onto a buttered plate; cool. Cut into pieces.

Yield: 2 dozen

TYBEE SALT WATER TAFFY

Everyone should enjoy at least one taffy pull before the summer's gone.
Salt water taffy does contain both salt and water, but the name actually comes
from the candy's place of origin, the New Jersey shore.

2 cups sugar	2 tablespoons butter or margarine
2 tablespoons cornstarch	2 teaspoons flavoring extract or
1 cup light corn syrup	1/2 teaspoon flavoring oil
3/4 cup water	Food coloring
1 teaspoon salt	

Grease a large marble slab or a large shallow baking pan. Combine the sugar and cornstarch in a saucepan and mix well. Add the corn syrup, water, salt and butter. Cook over medium heat until the sugar dissolves, stirring constantly; cover. Bring to a boil. Boil for 2 to 3 minutes; uncover. Boil until mixture reaches 266 degrees on a candy thermometer; do not stir. Remove from heat. Stir in the flavoring and food coloring. Pour onto the marble slab. Cool just until mixture can be handled. Pull the candy with greased hands until opaque and satiny. Pull into long ropes and cut into pieces. Wrap in waxed paper, twisting the ends to seal tightly. Store in an airtight container at room temperature.

Yield: 100 pieces

GRANNY'S PECAN PRALINES

Mixing a batch of pralines requires a lot of beating, but it's worth the effort for this very special treat.

2 cups sugar
1 cup half-and-half
1 teaspoon baking soda

$1/3$ cup butter
1 cup chopped pecans

Combine the sugar, half-and-half and baking soda in a saucepan and mix well. Cook over medium heat until mixture reaches 234 to 240 degrees on a candy thermometer, stirring constantly. Stir in the butter and pecans. Cook until butter is melted. Remove the pan from the heat. Place in a large bowl of cold water; do not allow any water into the mixture. Beat until mixture loses it luster. Drop by teaspoonfuls onto waxed paper.

Yield: 16 pralines

CHATHAM CRESCENT TURTLES

2 (6-ounce) packages vanilla caramels
2 tablespoons evaporated milk
2 cups pecan halves

1 (8-ounce) milk chocolate bar, broken into pieces
$1/3$ (4-ounce) bar paraffin, broken into pieces

Combine the caramels and evaporated milk in a double boiler. Cook until the caramels melt, stirring occasionally. Beat with a wooden spoon until creamy. Stir in the pecans. Drop by teaspoonfuls onto buttered waxed paper. Let stand for 15 minutes. Melt the chocolate and paraffin in a double boiler, stirring occasionally. Dip each candy with a wooden pick into the chocolate mixture. Place on waxed paper; let stand until hardened.

Yield: 4 dozen

Lyon's Long Room—Lyon a blacksmith and Liberty Boy, was the first tavern keeper to introduce cultural events, including a grand ball and a play. This was thanks largely to his wife, Sarah.

Excerpt from article of *Savannah News* 2/11/99

COOKBOOK ADVISORY COMMITTEE

Irving Victor, M.D.
Honorary Chairman

Beanie Barbee	Martha Hejka	Alice Noehren
Angela Brackett	Melanie Hurd	Robin Ogden
Nannette Cafiero	Gail Jones	Kay Orvin
Jane Cannon	Terri Verbeek-Jones	Anna Panicker
Sandy Chatfield	Mary Kelley	Bertie Skinner
Denise Chisner	Dottie Kluttz	Helen Steward
Patty Cullum	Dr. Toni McCullough	Bobbie Strong
Karen C. Davis	Linda Mehl	Linda Thompson
Cheryl Drwiega	Kathy Mermelstein	Pat Valenzano
Helen Marie Fleming	Cindy Murphy	Daphne Wall
Judy Freeman	Jo Ann Nelson	Sharon Yeager
Judy Hancock	Renee Newell	

Recipe Donors

Dottie Adams
Mary Adams
Tessie J. Adams
Dianne Albea
Vickie Ashley
Marcheta Austell
Nellie S. Bailey
Beanie Barbee
Johnathan Barrett
Louise Battle
Joette Bazemore
Lynda Beebe
Camille Bennett
Leslie Jones Bennett
Gloria Sheffield Betz
Courtney Brooke Blair, Esq.
Maxine Blair
Bodi's
Bonnie Boyette
Angela B. Brackett
Ann B. Brackett
Mae Brackett
Mickey Brady
Jan Brennan
Kimberly W. Brown
Carlyle Buelvas
Nannette Cafiero
Jane Cannon
Cancer Support Group
 • Susan Earman
 • Eileen Lemieux
 • Rick O'Connor
Care 65 Members
 • Sybil Barnett
 • Judy Downing
 • Louise Ferguson
 • Peggie B. Lane
 • Mary Lou Purvis
 • Jim Wilson
Helen Carellas
Dorothy Carnes
Sandy Chatfield
Becky Cheatham

Denise Chisner
Mrs. Thomas C. Clay
Lib Collins
Sandee Comer
Sandi Conti
Winell Cooler
Estelle Shumans Covenah
Leigh Craft
Judy Craig
Annette Cress
Patty Cullum
Alice M. Dailey
Evelle Dana
Sherry Danello
Anne Dauray
Karen C. Davis
Joan Day
Christy Dell 'Orco
Delphine DeMauro
Liz Dent
Dotsie Dewberry
Mary Dipman
Olive K. Dixon
Julie Dose
Katherine Driscoll
Cheryl Drwiega
Paul Drwiega
Rosine Drwiega
Kay Durden
Chandler Echols,
 Chef, Savannah Golf Club
Sr. Jeanette Edwards
Madge Edwards
Sheree Ernst
Suzanne Estus
Judy Farrell
Anne E. Fearon
Marianne Fields
Helen Marie Fleming
Dana B. Flood
Janice Forbes
Julie Foster
Sheila Fraser

Judy Freeman
Wendy Gillespie
Karoline Glatter
Richard Glendinning
Theresa P. Godbold
Sylvia Freedman Gold
Ellen S. Goodrich, R.N.
Barbara B. Granger
Robin Greco
Dixie W. Griffis
Cathie Hahn
Gay Hall
Lisa Hall
Judy Hancock
Nancy Hardee
Lillian M. Hardy
Sharon Harrison
Mindy Hartley
J. Harry Haslam, Jr.
Mrs. Falcon Hawkins
Delores Haynes
Betty Heard
Sr. Connie Heidewald, RSM
Margaret Heil
Kay Henderson
Bill Herrington
Theresa Hiers
JoAnne C. Hilker
Carolyn Hillis
Phyllis Hodges
Larry Hooks
Patsy Hopkins
Melanie Hurd
Susan Hurt
Minnie Ingram
Jean Jensen
Willine Johnson
Helen M. Johnson
Alice L. Johnston
Willine Johnston
Gail B. Jones
Sally Kehoe
Helen King Kelley

James W. Kelley
Mary Kelley
Kay Kennerty
Stuart "Bo" Kersey
Catherine D. Knox
Robyn Kretschmar
Betty Lane
Seleta Lee
Michelle S. Leech
Jane H. Lemon
Billigene Lewis
Dorothy M. Lockwood
Sr. Bernarda Loncon
Susan Mason Catering
Nina Massey
Lori Mastison
Ethel McAmis
Pauline McBride
Melissa McClary
Jim McCollum
Grace McCullough
Toni L. McCullough, M.D.
Bernard McDonough,
    Executive Chef
    The Ford Plantation
Linda Mehl
Louise Mills
Donna S. Mobley
Kimberly Mobley
Celeste Montgomery
Susan Morris
Johnnie Morrow
Connie Munn
Cheri G. Murray
Jo Ann Nelson
Paulette Nelson
Tammie Nelson
Renee Newell
Ruby Northcutt
Sharron Odom
Jackie Ogden
Robin Ogden
Michelle Ogle
Eunice S. Oglesby
Evelyn Oldfield
Kay Orvin

Ann Wenner Osteen
Brenda Outler
Katherine M. Owens
Steve Paavola
Jan Padgett
Anna Panicker
Mrs. Albert Parker
Evelyn Patrick
Sheryl Patwardhan
Amy Payne
Jean Peeples
Maria V. Perez
Janet Peters
Jane Philbrick
Cynthia Pollette
Shelley Prince
Ginger Pruden
Robyn Redding
Gloria Register
Elizabeth W. Ress
Traci Brackett Roach
Barbara C. Roberts
Laurie Ross
Mary Frances Roush
Jean Rousseau
Charles J. Russo Seafood
Evelyn Sanders
Savannah Candy Kitchen
Savannah News
Annabelle Schenk
Mrs. M.M. Schneider
Betsy Scully
Margarete Seagraves
Joyce Shedd
Mary Shelley
Katherine Sheppard
Debbie Shumans
Bertie Skinner
Barbara Danzi Smith
Susan Smith
Sophisticated Palate
Agnes Sorrells
Ria Sparkman
Rebecca Spell
Elaine Stahl
Linda Starr

Tina Stetson
Helen Steward
Pat Tanguay
Ann Tatum
Juanita Teasley
Dorothy H. Terry
Linda Thompson
Bill Tonkin
Debbie Townsend
Kay Tucker
Richard Underwood
University of Georgia
    Cooperative Extension Service
Debbie VanBrackle
Dr. Irving Victor
Mrs. Jules Victor, Jr. ("Noni")
David Wade
Charlotte C. Wall
Daphne Wall
Sequel B. Wall
Linda Dasher Wallace
Tammy Waller
Sr. Betty Walsh
Barbara Ann Walthour
Yvette Warnock
June Henderson Warren
Faye Watkins
Rachael Watkins
Kendra Watters
    Georgia Department of
    Agriculture
Mary L. Way
Jack W. Weathers
Julie Weddle
Angela Wells
Catherine Wells
Johnny Wells
Stephanie Wells
Kay C. West
Julia J. Williams
Earline Wilson
Delores Womack
Martha M. Woodbery
Tootie Wright
Dutch Young
Linda K. Zoller

INDEX

FROM BLACK TIE TO BLACKEYED PEAS
SAVANNAH'S SAVORY SECRETS

St. Joseph's Foundation of Savannah, Inc.
11705 Mercy Boulevard
Savannah, Georgia 31419
912/927-5117
877/264-2076 (toll free)

Please send _____ copies of FROM BLACK TIE TO BLACKEYED PEAS at $19.95 per book $ _____

Georgia residents add 6% sales tax at $1.20 per book $ _____

Postage and handling at $3.50 per book $ _____

Total $ _____

_____
Name

_____
Street Address

_____
City   State   Zip

_____
Telephone

Method of Payment: [   ] VISA   [   ] MasterCard   [   ] Discover   [   ] American Express
                  [   ] Check enclosed payable to St. Joseph's Foundation

_____
Account Number   Expiration Date

_____
Cardholder Name

_____
Signature

Photocopies will be accepted.